PENGUIN BOOKS

SOUND BITES

Alex Kapranos is the singer and guitarist of Franz Ferdinand. Before the success of the band, he spent more than a decade jumping between stints as a chef, wine waiter, kitchen porter, delivery driver, welder, promoter, college lecturer, and doley layabout: anything to generate the cash that his bands didn't.

Andrew Knowles is touring drummer and keyboards player with the band, and a graduate of the Glasgow School of Art.

Sound Bites

Eating on Tour with Franz Ferdinand

Alex Kapranos

Illustrations by
Andrew Knowles

PENGUIN BOOKS

PENGUIN BOOKS

Published by the Penguin Group
Penguin Group (USA) Inc., 375 Hudson Street, New York, New York 10014, U.S.A.
Penguin Group (Canada), 90 Eglinton Avenue East, Suite 700, Toronto, Ontario, Canada
M4P 2Y3 (a division of Pearson Penguin Canada Inc.)
Penguin Books Ltd, 80 Strand, London WC2R 0RL, England
Penguin Ireland, 25 St Stephen's Green, Dublin 2,
Ireland (a division of Penguin Books Ltd)
Penguin Group (Australia), 250 Camberwell Road, Camberwell,
Victoria 3124, Australia (a division of Pearson Australia Group Pty Ltd)
Penguin Books India Pvt Ltd, 11 Community Centre,
Panchsheel Park, New Delhi – 110 017, India
Penguin Group (NZ), cnr Airborne and Rosedale Roads, Albany,
Auckland 1310, New Zealand (a division of Pearson New Zealand Ltd)
Penguin Books (South Africa) (Pty) Ltd, 24 Sturdee Avenue,
Rosebank, Johannesburg 2196, South Africa

Penguin Books Ltd, Registered Offices:
80 Strand, London WC2R 0RL, England

First published in Great Britain by Fig Tree, an imprint of Penguin Books Ltd 2006
Published in Penguin Books (USA) 2006

Copyright © Alex Kapranos, 2006
Illustrations copyright © Andrew Knowles, 2006
All rights reserved

Portions of this book first appeared in issues of *The Guardian* (London).

1 3 5 7 9 10 8 6 4 2

Copyright © Alex Kapranos, 2006
All rights reserved

ISBN 978-0-14-303808-5
CIP data available

Printed in the United States of America

For Eleanor

CURIOUS NIBBLING - *tyne and wear*

It's late summer 1973, Washington new town, Tyne and Wear. I've been walking for a while now. Our new house smells amazing because the carpets have just been laid. This is our family's first house – we've been living with my grandparents until now – and it's still exciting to explore. I've been playing my new game: climbing to the top of the stairs and throwing myself back down. My chest and belly are scabby with carpet burns and I'm trembling with adrenalin. I push my face into the pile once more. It smells good. I need to explore. It's all so huge. There are no doors downstairs, so you can run in a big circle between the rooms. The kitchen is bright and unfriendly, but I can see Mam in the back garden talking to her new neighbour about the house-warming party she's having this evening. The best thing in the kitchen is the washing machine. It has big orange buttons and a purple plastic door, which turns the world purple when you squash your face against it and look through. I can't see much from that angle, just the cupboard door and a bit of lino, so I try to get inside. It looks good in there anyway – shiny like a spaceship with a million little holes to put your finger in. I put my head in and try to force the rest, but my shoulders are too big and the catch is hurting my arm, so I give up.

I wander back into the front room where there is a coffee table my granddad made. He smells of Woodbines and can make anything. It is covered in pretty-coloured glass bowls filled with snacks for the party, some of which I recognize, some I don't. More exploring. I'm curious to find out what tastes good. Crisps do – I know that already, so I eat them, enjoying the salt and the crunchy bites. A very different bite goes with the pink and white marshmallows. They're soft and you can put more in your mouth than you'd think. I've learned a good trick with them – if you do a sort of sicky burp move with your stomach, you can bring them back into your mouth and chew them a second time. I like doing this because they taste different second time around. Then there are orange squares on a stick with yellow squares. The yellow squares are pineapple chunks and are tasty, a bit like sweets, but not quite as good. Mam lets me drink the juice from the tin when we have them for tea. The orange squares are cheese. I suck on one, even though I know it won't be good. It isn't, so I put it back in the bowl. Grown-ups' food. Horrible. On another square, there's a little onion. That's good — crunchy and squirty-tasting. I eat more, making sure I leave the orange squares behind. Tomatoes. They're disgusting. There's a bowl of slices. It's the slimy green pips that are worst. Still, I'm feeling curious. I want to know if I can ever like this stuff. No way. I can't even swallow it. I spit it out and hide it under a cushion. There is no way I will like that taste. Ever. I'm feeling full, but it's fun.

There's a bowl of things I've not seen before. They're almost the colour of crisps and have a weird smell that makes the back of my tongue clench against the opening of my throat. I pick one up. It's hard, so I roll it between my palms before putting it in my mouth. It's salty and crunchy and . . . No. Something's wrong. My mouth itches. It's tingling and itchy and my throat feels like a cactus. I stagger away from the table. I spit the last bit from my mouth. I'm starting to drool. I can't stop the slobber. It's pouring from the corners of my mouth like a left-on tap. Now my stomach is doing a weird thing. It's wobbling like I'm on my swing, but in a bad way. It's a bit scary. No — it's really scary. Something bad is happening and I have no idea what it is. I start moaning. 'Mam!' Where is she? 'Mam!' She'll help. My stomach clamps, like a strangling fist. I throw my stomach contents in an arc across the carpet. 'Mam!' I start to run. Another arc. 'Mam!' I slip in the sludge of half-digested nibbles. 'Mam!' I run between every room, tramping secondhand crisps, pickled onions, marshmallows and pineapple into the new carpet. My beautiful twenty-four-year-old mother appears like an angel. I run with arms stretching out for comfort. I'm scooped into the air. Everything's all right. She holds me under the armpits with her left arm. My trousers are down. She swings. I rock from the first blow. My tiny arse stings. I puke down her arm. She's shouting something about carpets, parties and a little shit.

Later I sit at the foot of the stairs, too exhausted to sob any more than an odd hiccup of sorrow. My mother is still angry, scrubbing the last traces before her guests arrive. The smell of sick can't hide behind this new smell called Dettol and decorates the air like sorrow. I don't know the word, but I know I'm allergic to peanuts. I know I don't like tomatoes or cheese. I know I like crisps and marshmallows. The sobbing subsides to exhausted calm. I feel empty and good, everything seems clear and easy to understand. I think about the food – its flavours and how it felt in my mouth, how different each thing was, how it could taste of joy, revulsion or painful destruction. I don't think of it as a thing that stops me from being hungry. I know it is much more than that. Food is an adventure.

PREP WORK - *glasgow*

The greatest preparation I had for touring with a band was working as a chef alongside Bob Hardy in a Glasgow kitchen. We wielded knives, hot fat and broccoli inches from each other in a small, very hot, windowless kitchen through double shifts from 9 a.m. till 1 a.m. We poured cooking brandy down our throats and scorn upon the waiters. Sharing a claustrophobic tour-bus, like we do now, seems easy – tame in comparison.

I worked in a lot of restaurants and kitchens before Franz Ferdinand, and that was the greatest. The head chef, Martin Tiblitski, was as rock and roll as anyone I've ever met in a band, but he was also cool-headed. Saturday-night service was soundtracked by the Stooges and the Velvet Underground rather than the barking of an egomaniac. It was from him that we learned that a great group dynamic is worth more than the merits of any individual, that langoustine fight back when you kill them and that boiled marrow bones make the *jus* that glues a good menu together.

So, I've had a call from the *Guardian*. They want me to write about what I eat on the road. Well, most of the time, it's boring – I grab whatever snacks are lying around. I shove crisps, ageing sandwiches and cold pizza into my gob between sound-checks, gigs and sitting on a bus drunk. But I'm not going to tell them that. I'll tell them about the weird stuff – the freaky stuff you don't get on Alexandra Parade, Dennistoun; the flavours I didn't know existed; the dives and the glamour.

Over the last couple of years, this group has taken me around the world two and a half times. Sometimes I eat appallingly. Sometimes I eat phenomenally well. I never eat predictably.

I've chipped my molars on tiny pearls from mussels in Brussels. Three days ago, I ate a Sumo wrestler's hotpot in Shibuya, then walked to my hotel through a plague of rats. I've been poisoned by *molé* from a Mexico City convent. I witnessed the failed taming of the Pacific Oyster in Portland. I realized that the finest fast food in the world is on the streets of Athens. I munched a slice of fishbrain bread from Finland (tastier than you'd imagine, but not as interesting). I discovered that sea urchin is the only food I've ever put in my mouth and physically not been able to swallow, while sitting in the restaurant that was the setting for the Samurai sword slaughter in *Kill Bill*. I've walked Cake Lover's Lane in Melbourne and dunked Polish donuts and Key Lime pie in Brooklyn. I chewed alligator sausage in New Orleans, unable to leave the restaurant until the police had finished pouring tear gas into the apartment two floors above us to diffuse a hostage situation. I drank beetroot juice until my sweat ran red. I learned how to toast from Georgians in Moscow and ate blinis in the St Petersburg dining room that was formerly the offices of the KGB. Yes, food is still an adventure.

PURPLE GORAM - *new york*

It hits the wing-collared dinner shirt like fresh blood on
blotting paper. I feel nauseous. Andy Goram is saturated with
Châteauneuf du Pape. I'm nineteen and have just lost my job as
a wine waiter at a large banqueting hall in Glasgow. Goram is
Rangers' goalkeeper. Half of the wine waiters love him. The
others support Celtic and despise him. There's a wee bit of
rivalry between the two Glasgow teams. I have been given his
table because, as a Greek Orthodox Sunderland supporter, I
prefer neither. The guy waiting the table next to mine prefers
Celtic. I passed around the table, calmly pouring, unfazed by
Goram's fame. I reached his glass, unaware of the silent Celtic
type behind me. Unaware until he firmly grabbed my elbow
and shoved it.

It's September, and I'm sitting outside a Greek restaurant on
48th Street when my two friends arrive pissed, grinning with
Mojitos, and order a bottle of rosé. The wine waiter appears
from the shadows, flicks half an inch into the glass. My
friend's telling a good joke, hits the punch line and knocks it
back, nodding at the waiter. We laugh. He fills our glasses.
Another joke. Another swig. I take a sip of mine. It's wrong.
They've almost finished their glasses. I take another sip.
Definitely wrong: like mouldy old tent with mushrooms and
vinegar. Corked. They top up again, too drunk to notice or
care. I can't drink it, but I'd love a glass of wine right now, if
only to communicate on the same level. I still have that stupid
British habit of avoiding complaining whenever I can. When I
murmur to the wine waiter, it comes out sounding more like an
apology than a complaint. 'Is this supposed to taste like this?'
He doesn't taste it. He sniffs it and disappears. The rotten
bottle is replaced with a fresh one. My friends don't notice.

He slinks away between the tables like a breeze of suave discretion. God, I was not suave. I was not discreet, as I stood gormless before the purple Goram twelve years ago.

My job-title was grander than my capabilities. There were ten bottles of wine on the menu and I could tell customers which ones were red and which ones were white. After a few weeks I learned which were sweet or dry, French or Italian. I also learned how to collect the half-empty bottles at the end of the night and fill them with a funnel for the next night, how to tie a bow-tie (there's a bit of Velcro behind the knot), how to set up a boxing ring and how to blow smoke into the air-vent of the staffroom bogs when smoking a joint.

My first experience with wine was at the Dafni wine festival in Greece. On visits to my Greek grandparents, everyone drank wine, usually retsina, with meals. I tried it when they weren't looking but hated the cold, unfriendly taste. I was about eight when we went to Dafni. It was picturesque: lights hung from the cypress and olive trees, there were little wooden bridges over ponds and giant barrels of different Greek wines. Visitors paid a few drachmas for a glass, then wandered around, tasting whatever they wanted. My parents were happily distracted, so my brother and I went off exploring. We borrowed a couple of glasses and helped ourselves from the barrels. Everything tasted foul — bitter and impossible to swallow. We spat it out, on to the dust and down our T-shirts. Then we found the black stuff. It was red, but so dark it looked black. It didn't taste like the other wine. It tasted of raisins — very sweet, tasty, juicy raisins. We filled our tumblers, and it tumbled down into our bellies. Everything was very funny. Our voices sounded funny. The lights were bright in a lovely way. We saw a fat German man with a big moustache fill up a beer glass with wine and down it like beer. This was so funny that we couldn't stop laughing. He disappeared, but we couldn't stop. We fell on our knees, as stitches developed. We were laughing so hard, it was almost impossible to swallow much more of this magnificent, sweet juice. When our parents found us, we were lying on our backs in the dust, sobbing with laughter, barely able to breathe. I fell asleep on the dizzy drive back to Athens and woke up the next day wondering why my brother was hitting me hard on the head with his Tonka truck. It was my first hangover.

A cowboy is standing outside Las Manitas. His beard is grizzled beneath a straw Stetson and wraparound shades. He is wearing a boob tube, convincingly filled with a spectacular set of implants. Apart from his spurred boots, the only other thing he is wearing is a pair of luminous pink Speedo swimming trunks. Also convincingly filled. This is Austin, and the cowboys here are not like those in the rest of Texas.

Las Manitas is on Congress between the Capitol building and Lake Austin. Lake Austin isn't a lake: it's a river. There is a bridge over it, which is home to thousands of bats which swarm out every day at dusk. Tourists gather on the riverbanks to watch with vendors selling ice cream and cold drinks. It opens only for breakfast and lunch but has a reputation for the best Tex-Mex in Texas. Heavy fans beat the thick air, and my thighs stick to the cracked green-vinyl seat. The scruffy, beige lino squares are worn to the concrete in furrows from the frantic passing of waiters. Freshly squeezed orange thuds on to my table in a plastic

tumbler the size of a small wastepaper bin. On the menu are Huevos Rancheros, Chilaquiles (*Verdes* or *Rojos*) and Plato de Chorizo. The only beans are black or refried. I ask a Texan if they ever eat kidney beans: 'Euw. Gross.'

Kidney beans seem to be a British interpretation of Mexican food, like mayonnaise with sushi or lasagne and chips. I order Migas Especiales con Hongos, which is eggs scrambled with tortilla strips and mushrooms under a heavy blanket of cheese and red chilli sauce. There is a pool of black beans and a glorious dod of guacamole, light with lime and coriander, on the side. It is perfect breakfast food: homely and reassuring, with enough piquancy to wake you up.

Las Manitas, or Little Hands, is slang for a gang of mates, and that's what this place is run by: a group of friends who, as Mexican students, couldn't find what they wanted to eat in the local supermarkets. It's informal. To get to the restroom, you pass through the kitchen. Huge, blackened pots hang from chains bolted to the ceiling. The staff are oblivious to you, expressionless as they roll their hundredth enchilada, sweat at the broiler or hoist buckets of greasy crockery over their heads. Above the doors are two hand-painted signs, one reading YES, the other NO. I choose YES, and I'm back on Congress. It's 108° Fahrenheit. Today we will play the outdoor Austin City Limits festival and it will be the hottest I have ever been on stage. I will feel as ungainly as a brontosaurus, my limbs heavy with heat, dragging a few seconds behind the requests of my brain. The cowboy has gone and, as my shirt and trousers scrape my sweating skin, I wonder if Speedos and a boob tube are just a practical choice.

His face is grey with fear. Anxiety flickers across the eyes. They dart around the table, bouncing off the expectant gazes surrounding him. Resolve hardens the tendons around the jaw. He picks up a shell. It's tinged with a delicate green at the edge. The little grey creature glistens under the candlelight. He tips it past the lips. He chews. There's a grimace. He chews some more, rolling it to the molars on the other side. There's a desperate furrowing of the eyebrows and a swallow. The swallow becomes a gag. A grey gob shoots out. It's caught on the shell. He stares at it. With a glare of defiance, he tips it into his mouth again. It's straight back out. Paul, our drummer, has never tried oysters before.

He is adventurous and loves food. This tour, he has been compiling a chart of burgers he's eaten around the world, documenting them with a complex rating system based upon appearance, condiments, texture, presentation and novelty. Novelty could be guacamole, a fried egg or jalapenos — anything out of the ordinary. The top of the list is a tie between Freshness Burger of Tokyo and In 'n' Out Burger of LA.

Food on the road has been a bit dismal recently. On the shores of the Great Salt Lake there was nothing but a box of stale bagels. The venue was wonderful, though: a bizarre jumble of minarets and towers called the Great Saltair Pavilion, built in the late nineteenth century by the Mormon church as a 'Coney Island of the West' where bathers could bob unsinkable in the dense salt water. The lake stinks. I don't know how long it took the tourists to work that out, but they stopped coming after the thirties, and the pavilion fell into disuse. The sand has a crust of salt which cracks as you walk across it. Dead birds litter the beach and a power station smokes on the far shore. It is an unearthly landscape, dramatic, inspiring and unsettling. The guys who ran it were a loose punk collective with an approach, completely at odds with the corporate Clearchannel uniformity found in most of the larger venues in the States. Other than those bagels, it's been Subway. We're in Seattle and feel like something special. Ocean Aire is recommended. The linen is stiff, but the atmosphere's not. We drink Bloody Caesars: like a Mary but with clam juice. A huge prawn hangs off the lip of the glass. Rose, our waitress, describes Westcott Bay oysters as buttery with a copper aftertaste. Part of the appeal of oysters is the ceremony. The shucking, the loosening of the flesh and the drizzle of lemon create a sense of occasion.

After the meal, Paul said that this was what made him want to try them – he felt he was missing out on something decadent and special. I ask what he didn't like about them.

'The texture really, I didn't like. It was tough like squid, but gritty. I wasn't that mad on the flavour and I literally couldn't swallow it. I had this horrible thing in my mouth I wanted to get out immediately.'

I ask him if he would try them again.

'I've got to an age where if there's something I haven't tried, there's probably a good reason for it.'

Pray: Ta Da Ki Ma Su. Thank you, Mother Earth, I accept and adopt your gifts. They will thrive through my body.

My body is not thriving. I'm trying to sit cross-legged on a straw mat. I've somehow jammed a knee under the foot-high table. Sensation has gone. A plastic tombstone is rammed into my ribs. I read the prayer at the top of the photocopied menu.

We're on the Mission, San Francisco, in the Country Station Sushi Café. Os Mutantes, the Brazilian psychedelics, shimmer from the speakers. We're digging the wasabi head rush. This is not like any other sushi restaurant. This is chaos. Clutter is not associated with sushi, but it dominates this tiny restaurant. Every surface is covered with random detritus: shells, Ramones and Fluxus posters, thousands of photographs, plastic Santas, plastic Satans, washboards and beautiful hand-painted kites. It is the converse of the clean surgical lines and order of the standard sushi environment. The specials are scribbled on a piece of corrugated card ripped from an Asahi box. We get some of Mother Earth's Dizzaster Rolls: Tyfoon (salmon and mango), Hurcane (tuna masago) and Beaty and the Beast (eel papaya). Crabs go crunch, soft-shelled, fried and halved, like a swarm of tarantulas emerging from a porcelain pool. Devour them before they get you. They're delicate and crispy. I'm overwhelmed. This tastes *fine*. Daintily fanned avocado cloaks red snapper, but the highlight is the eel – smoked sweet darkness.

Elephantine bulbs of garlic hang from the frame of a nearby door, upon which is pinned a note: 'Toilit is sick. Pleas no paper. Be gentel pleas.' There is a doodle of a toilet with a pained expression on its face. Percussion instruments made of bottle

tops, beads and what look like giant tumours lie scattered between us. This place is infused with an anarchic joy.

Then we're back on Mission. U-Save Discount Thrift. Fred's Liquor. Checks Cashed. Payday Loans. Hotel: Daily Rates. A figure in slept-in leathers rollerblades up to us with an acoustic guitar. He sings a desperate 'Dust in the Wind'. He looks and sounds like a starving seal. The reek of idealism and hedonism soured by crack and Forties overwhelms the faint scent of incense drifting from the café.

It's odd to eat sushi amongst disorder, but the Country Station is friendly and unintimidating. The most intimidating sushi restaurant I've been to is Sushi Nozawa in Studio City, LA. The chef wears an eye patch and has no respect for the judgement of his customers. A sign reads: 'Today's Special: Trust Me.' Painted above the door of the back kitchen are the words 'Trust Me'. A picture frame contains a three-dimensional boat. The name of the boat is *Trust Me*. A red State of Arizona number plate is embossed with 'Trust Me.' Daffy Duck is painted on the wall. 'Trust Me,' he says. A piece of fabric is embroidered with the words 'Don't Think: Just Eat.' He fixes you with his working eye. He dares you to think. He dares you to question. he holds a knife the size of a cutlass. You trust him.

CHOP AND CHANGE-*new york*

As you step down from West 36th into the mahogany half-light of Keen's Chop House, you descend into another Manhattan, a moment buried over a hundred years ago, preserved like a dustbin in the *Blue Peter* garden. The dark wood, linen and silverware are in tune with the refined simplicity of the menu. There are no show-off celebrity-chef creations. Instead, there is a mutton chop. You never see mutton on a modern menu. It has picked up ugly connotations, tainted like 'lard', 'tripe' or 'boiling fowl', suggesting something our grandparents' parents ate because they didn't know better. Mutton is what lamb turns into after its first birthday. Somehow, there is a stigma attached to eating an old sheep, but not an old cow.

There is a lobster holding tank by our table. They are clambering on top of each other, as if making a great escape. A starched waiter dips a clamping device known as a Cosby Grabber into the tank and grasps a blue monster by the thorax. One of my companions loves lobsters. Not to eat, but for their unsung sophistication. She tells me how they link claws as they walk along the seabed, like lovers holding hands. How, when they meet, they run a claw over bumpy backs to find out each other's age and where they grew up. They are monogamous and live well into their fifties. 'I feel uncomfortable eating anything older than me,' she says, and I don't feel like lobster tonight. There's hypocrisy in my compassion. I have slaughtered thousands of crustaceans in kitchens. Brutally. Crabs sense death. Five of them on their backs, still dazed from the fridge. Between their legs is a frilled flap protecting their genitalia. Little on the guys, big on the girls. Rip it off. Now they know. Flailing in fear and agony. Cleaver cleaves. Precise. Split the shell. Tear the legs. Clean the dead man's fingers. Toss in the wok. Compassion? What? Was that an order for table ten?

Salivating with carnivorous hypocrisy, I slice into my mutton chop. The flesh is rich: regal crudity in the velvet shadows of this archaic and elegant setting.

There's a collection of clay pipes that belonged to famous diners who ate, drank and smoked in Keen's, including Theodore Roosevelt's. At that time, you would take your pipe to your favourite place and they would look after it for you so you didn't break it when you were staggering home through Central Park after a heavy night. One of the lovely things about Keen's is that there is no music. I hate it when restaurant owners impose their taste on their diners. The best background noise in any restaurant anywhere is the warm murmur of people enjoying their food and each other's company. The worst background noise is the modern muzak, bland house wash that appeared in the mid-nineties in hip minimalist bars and restaurants.

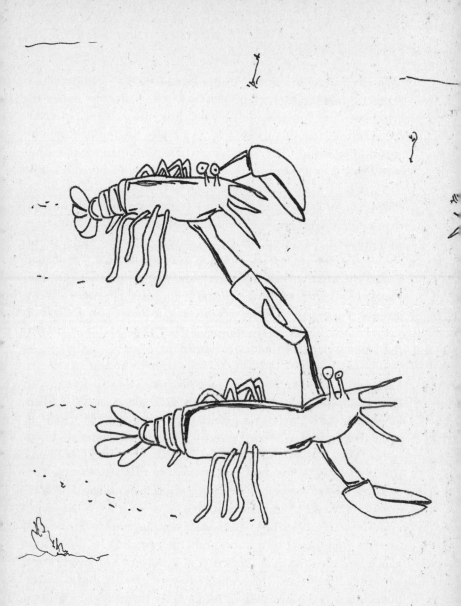

8.45 a.m., October 2000. I'm not hungover, I'm still drunk. I stagger down the back stairs, thirty kilos of marrow bones in my arms. I'm a commis chef. It's a daily routine. They're in flat cardboard boxes. Blood seeps from a soggy corner through my apron and whites. They clatter as I tip them into a roasting tray. Once they are browned, I dump them into a pot and fill it with water. I grunt with a kitchen porter (KP) as we lift it on to the warm stove, to join the pot I left yesterday and the pot that's been simmering for two days. All proportions are exaggerated. An eight-year-old could bathe comfortably among the bones. Staring into the monstrous pots, I feel like I'm in the kitchen of a filthy giant who picks gristle from his rotten teeth with saplings. I strain the juice from the oldest pot and reduce it to two litres of rich, intense *jus*. Formless carrots and dead bayleaves cling to the desolate bones remaining. I don't consider eating them.

8.45 p.m., October 2005. I'm not drunk, I'm still hungover. 'You MUST go to Blue Ribbon.' 'It's THE place in NYC.' 'The Pu-Pu Platter NEVER disappoints.' 'It's where CHEFS go when they finish shifts.' 'The marrow bone and marmalade is AWESOME.' 'Blah blah blah.' On this US tour I've been barraged by New Yorkers recommending this restaurant. I'm curious. Marrow bones? Do dogs know something I don't? Stars and Stripes sag from a flag on the ceiling. At the table opposite, a man in his fifties wears a homemade Stars and Stripes jumper. It's tight under the arms. 'Are there any specials?' I ask the enthusiastic young waiter. 'Yes, but if I tell you, they'll beat me.' He's replaced by an equally enthusiastic but slightly smoother model. As he talks lovingly through the menu, it's obvious that not only does he eat this food regularly, but it's the reason he works here. 'Would you recommend the marrow bone?' 'That,' he says, 'is a VERY good choice.'

It arrives sawn into three segments, served with toast. The marmalade looks like Branston pickle. A wooden fork is stuck in the marrow. It's the type you eat your chips with on Blackpool Pleasure Beach. I scoop out a dollop. Glistening. Pink. Gelatinous. 'That's truly gross,' chimes my companion. It reminds me of placenta. I spread it on the toast. It tastes ... good ... very good – homely, comforting. It would be perfect for convalescing. I can see why our canine pals dig the bone, but I can't stop my stomach from quivering with suspicion.

Jus is one of those secrets hidden from domestic kitchens by chefs. It's what sets restaurants aside from homemade food. Who could be bothered to boil huge pots of cow bones for three days in their kitchen for some glorious gravy? My first kitchen job was as a KP, aged eighteen, in a place in Fort William called McTavish's kitchens. I lost my virginity on the staffroom floor. The head chef was a '69 skinhead called Martin who had oversized canine teeth that made him look like a crew-cut nosferatu. We got on because I used to listen to the Specials and the Skatalites when I scrubbed the pots. A lot of chefs start out as KPs. One day you arrive for work, expecting to scrape vegetables and scrub pots, but the commis hasn't turned up, so there you are – standing in someone else's baggy whites, anxiety and expectancy perspiring on your brow. My first task was to prepare cow carcases for the *jus* pot. I would take a cleaver to horror-show ribcages. My second job was to rip the Fallopian tubes out of boiling fowl. They're the has-beens of the factory farm, past their optimum laying capacity, only fit for consumption as staff lunch at a large Fort William restaurant. Waves of nausea hit me as I first put my hand into the cavity and pulled out the mess of half-formed eggs and bad stench. After a couple of hundred, you didn't notice.

Martin was a good head chef, but a little brutal. On one of my first shifts, I sliced my finger for the first time. I was using someone else's knife and couldn't really control it. The tip of my finger was flapping in a useless gush of blood. 'I know how to stop that bleeding,' grinned Martin, his fangs hanging over his lower lip as he grabbed my hand. He jabbed it into the large bowl of salt that sat in the middle of the central prep area, jolting an instant sensation of electrocution through my arm. It was as if a thousand volts was passing through my finger. I pulled it out, crystals congealing around the wound like tiny rubies. 'Ha ha. You won't cut THAT finger again in a hurry,' he said. He was right. I cut the other ones instead.

'It is a convention left over from Christian times.' In perfect RP, the receptionist explains that everything is shut in Paris. Today is a Sunday. The hotel is at the foot of Montmartre, by Rue des Martyrs, one of the finest Parisian food streets which, when it is busy, stimulates every sense. Each end is sealed, and there is a throng of shoppers prodding the produce and arguing with the stallholders. There are a few interesting buildings. If you look up as you walk to the bottom of the street, there is a ramshackle, shed-like building made of corrugated tin. If you look through the dusty windows, you can make out the shadows of huge papier-maché heads. At the top of the hill, there is the magnificent boulangerie Armand de Montel. There is always an intimidating queue, but the rhubarb *tartes* are wonderful. In the sandstone around the door are letters etched in Roman script: Á *la Renaissance — pains français & étrangers. Pains chauds pour diners, pâtisserie fine & assortie, commands pour la ville.* On the opposite side of the street is the Rose Bakery. It's supposed to be an English tea room, but they get it wrong in a spectacularly successful French way. You can sit outside on aluminium chairs that look as if Philippe Starck made them. The brunch and particularly the quiche are good. Best of all, you get to sit outside and stare and be stared at. I'm unashamedly nosey and love it. People are fascinating, and checking them out is expected in Paris. They stare right back. I check out the old woman with the worn-out flip-flops while forking a roasted parsnip. I stare at the newly engaged couple, rings glinting in the low sunlight. I scoop chickpeas into my mouth. A kid dressed head to foot in denim wobbling past on stabilizers. A shuffling man with disappointed eyebrows, his neck swallowing his tiny chin. A skater clattering by on his back wheels. All meet the gaze unfazed as I swallow my broccoli. The Versace woman at the next table drops petits-fours into the yapping mouth of a Snowy-from-*Tintin* lapdog. If you stare at someone in a street in Glasgow, it's an invitation for a fight. If you stare at someone in Paris, it's because you want to look at them.

Last time I was here, it was a Friday and spectacular. A cheeky *chien* trotted perkily down the middle of the *rue* with a baguette in his mouth. *Champignons*, wild like delicate orchids, tumbled from wooden boxes. Monsters of the deep with claws akimbo lay splayed on ice. Hares hung from hooks over coils of sausage and chickens that were thick-boned from healthy life. *Fromageries* oozed their heady pungency. *Pâtisseries* seduced me with the sweet scent of *tartes*, a crumb of which could exhaust your tastebuds for a week. Today is a Sunday. Rue des Martyrs is desolate.

At nightfall, the options are still bleak. Chez Jean, one of the greatest restaurants I've ever eaten at, is yards away on Rue Saint Lazare. It is shut. Of course. It is open for a total of twenty-three hours a week. Not weekends. I cross Pigalle under the glow of busty neon silhouettes, up the narrow, cobbled Rue Piemontes. There are a lot of corners. Each is occupied. The occupants look like they're dressed for the Occupation: veil, fishnets, fag and a clutch bag – heritage whores in a historical re-enactment. On Rue Aristide Bruant, Le Taroudant II is bright like my grandparents' living room – homely and welcoming, but a bit more Moroccan. Everybody smokes. Between courses. During courses. It is run by a couple in their mid fifties. M. Taroudant has a clipped moustache and a silver teapot in his hand. He brings the spout to the lip of a

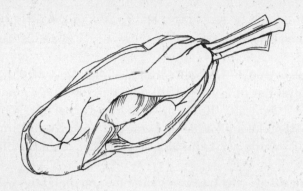

cup and raises his arm, slicing an arc of mercury through the air. He is stoic with the confidence of a practised and understated showman. Mme. Taroudant brings me a Tagine d'agneau. The clay is black with splashes hardened by the unforgiving fire, the ghosts of a thousand meals. Prunes fall from the stone. *L'agneau* falls from the Y-shaped bone. I can't tell what kind of bone. I try to summon some knowledge of *agneau* anatomy, but give up. I don't care. It is magnificent. Thank God for the Parisians who are unaware of a convention left over from Christian times.

'So what exactly is a gizzard?' My band-mates want to know what's in Salade de gésiers, other than leaves and dressing.

'It's a fleshy pouch in which birds mash up seeds with bits of grit before digesting them.' I'm not making this sound like much of a delicacy. 'Honestly, they're very tender, like the oysters from the underside of a chicken – you know... the bit Henry VIII would eat, before discarding the rest of the bird.'

Ordering Salade Niçoise, they nod encouragingly; the way my former colleagues did when, at the age of thirty, I said I was leaving my job as a lecturer to sing in a pop group. I don't mind. I'm a gastro-adventurer. Or something.

We're sitting outside at a rickety café table. Sunglasses and scarves are *à la mode* with diners on this bright November day. We're by the sprawling Parisian fleamarket in Clignancourt. Stalls selling counterfeit Sean Paul and G-Unit clothes seem somehow magical. It's because of the scent of roasting chestnuts that hangs in the air. There are few foods left which are truly seasonal and fewer which enhance a sense of season more than chestnuts on a brazier. As you crack the blackened shell to raid the hot fluffy sweetness inside, squirts of primal saliva fill your hunter-gatherer's mouth. This is a predominantly Arab area. Behind the glass of a rôtisserie over the road, thirty chickens drip their richness on to golden potatoes in a tray. The birds waiting to be roasted boast two proud rosettes, reading *'Volaille de Normand contrôlée'* and *'Société contrôlée de viande Halal'*. This relationship seems eerily symbiotic after nine nights of race rioting. There's discontent amongst French Arabs, who feel they are not assimilated into or accepted by French society.

As we wait for our food, a mangy pigeon with a gnarled red stump picks the dried gristle from a chicken bone that must have been in the gutter since last night. I steel my stomach. Nothing's going to spoil my lunch: I'm a gastro-adventurer. Or something. Bored, the pigeon flaps off into the path of a Vespa and tumbles to the tarmac, winged. We gasp collectively. It looks at us with a dazed 'What I do wrong?' expression, staggers towards us and under the wheel of a Renault. There's a simultaneous crunch and pop, like a kid jumping on an empty juice carton. It's gone — replaced by a flat mess of bones, guts and feathers. The gastro-adventurer's gésiers arrive, nestling deep, rare pink, between frilly leaves.

The first time I tried Salade de gésiers was with the parents of my friend Helen. They are fabulous Francophiles, who drove us around the South of France, putting new flavours in our mouths, with unpretentious enthusiasm and love for the country's food. Robert used to smuggle potatoes and seeds across the Channel so he could grow a bit of France in his allotment back in Glasgow. 'Gizzard' is an unappetizing word. It sounds like a twisted, poisonous organ, conjuring images of Alex and his Droogs or Kenny Everett — not something to eat — but because they tucked in without pausing to wrinkle their noses in distaste, it seemed like a natural and probably enjoyable thing to try.

THE LOVE OF A GOOD CURRY - *glasgow*

After five and a half weeks of touring the USA, all I wanted when I got back to Britain was the love of a good curry. I made the mistake of going to Brick Lane. I had some astounding and exotic meals in the States, but no good Indian food. It became the vivid taste of homesickness — a distant desire, unattainable. Not HP sauce, Tetley tea or Yorkshire puddings, but Saag Paneer. Within three hours of landing at Heathrow, I was being hounded by the Curry Criers of the Lane, touting specials and shouting about why their place is so much better than the seemingly identical place next door. With food, coercion is danger and recommendation is all. Still, I was jet-lagged and delirious with happiness at the prospect of a spicy treat. There was a voice within murmuring that I should get the bus up to Stoke Newington and go to Rasa on Church Street, where you can taste the love and affection in every bite, but it was drowned out by the sound of the Balti Barkers. The much-anticipated feast was slightly below mediocre. I was lucky.

Tonight, I'm at Mother India's Café in Glasgow. The prospects are good. In 1995, Monir Mohammed noticed that the food he liked to eat at home and the food served in curry restaurants weren't the same. At home, it was exploding with fresh ginger, garlic, cardamom and coriander. In the restaurants, it was bright with food colouring, but dull, thin and vicious in flavour. Figuring that other people might want a bit of what he wanted, he opened Mother India. The café serves, in tapas style, small bowls of delicacies to be shared rather than one heavy mound you can't finish, making for a much more sociable experience. It's how eating out should be, comparing, sharing and discussing your food, rather than the selfish ploughing through the portions which is particular to the UK and North America. Six years ago, I worked for Mother India, delivering across the city in an old Fiat. The only reliable thing about the car was that the sunroof would leak if it rained. It rains quite often in Glasgow. The smells of damp Panda and hot spices in brown paper are neighbours in my memory. I gained a cabby's knowledge of the city's shortcuts and was paid £10 a night, but the real reason I did it was for the free curry at the end of the evening. Something I never got when touring the USA in a Rock 'n' Roll Band.

I go back to the café every time I come home to Glasgow. I love the idea of a meal being the ultimate social experience — leaning over the table to swap spoonfuls of flavours with your friends. I've always hated the head-down selfishness of old-fashioned dining. It's as if the food is a prisoner on the plate waiting only for the final escort by fork to the execution chamber of your mouth: a joyless and private experience.

I was very fond of the Fiat Panda I used to drive for Mother India. They are amazing cars – 750ccs of efficiency and seats like deckchairs. I drove it with some friends to Blackpool in the summer of 2000. We ate chips and mushy peas on the beach, rode the rollercoaster and squashed coins on the tram tracks. At sunset we headed home. When we were halfway up the motorway, the radiator cracked. We had to stop at every Little Chef and Welcome Rest service station on the way back home and beg them for cups of hot water to top it up. I couldn't afford to fix it, but carried on driving it for a couple of weeks after that trip. It finally blew up spectacularly on the M8, oil and water gushing from the exhaust and black smoke billowing from the bonnet.

FORLORN FRIDGE - *glasgow*

The food has been in the fridge for two and a half years. I'm back in my Glasgow flat. I'm not home often. Everything is as it was when I left for Sweden, in the summer of 2003, to record our first album. A packet of vine leaves, a jar of chilli paste, something that looks like dripping and a carton of orange. All still there. Tonight I'm eating out. Again.

I rattle West of Dennistoun in a cab, along the fizzing spray of motorway, a mile of dirty concrete cast across the city like a slice of gristle through the Glaswegian heart. Clattering off at Charing Cross, we pull up in the dead-end of Argyll Street, Finnieston. Brutalist blocks of flats loom from the gentle rain. The scaffolding-clad Kingston Bridge dominates the skyline. Sodium half-light ripples off puddles, black as blood at midnight. A draggled whippet shambles past in a fluorescent orange coat. I'm eating at the oldest, noblest restaurant in town.

The Buttery was built in the mid-nineteenth century. Originally a wine merchant's cellar, it expanded over the next hundred years and gained a reputation for its food. In the late 1960s, Glasgow's town planners tore up the city. The tenements of Finnieston were razed. The only building left standing was the Buttery. Apparently, it survived because the architects and contractors ripping up the city didn't want to lose their favourite haunt. A Masonic plaque on the wall outside, bright under a lonely spotlight, may be another clue to its survival.

I'm eating with a friend who updates me with six months of gossip, asks the waiter for another one of those crispy things and whispers that she feels awkward as a socialist for eating somewhere like this. She's distracted by a bottle of heavy red,

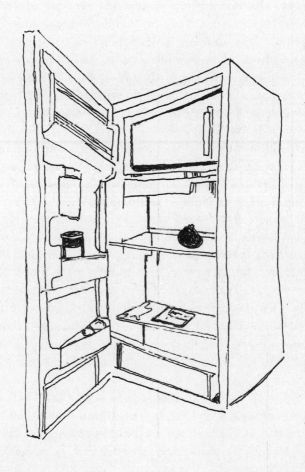

and we lean back into the padding of our chairs. The peaceful warmth envelops us like a good library with the reassurance of ancient oak, leather and stained glass. Like the best of Scottish menus, the Buttery's is an *entente cordiale* of French and Caledonian cuisine: Loin of Ayrshire Lamb and Provençal Vegetables. Smoked Confit of French Hen with Spiced Haggis – the chieftain of the pudding race, maligned in undeserved disgrace. I love this bag of sheep bits and oatmeal. In an age of gourmet sausages and head-to-tail eating, it is worthy of a higher place in the culinary canon. The aromatic richness is balanced by one of the greatest textures to greet the teeth, a gentle bite between your porcelain. While haggis now regularly appears on the menus of good Scottish restaurants, it is still treated with suspicion outside the country. I can't recommend it enough. It is a true regional delicacy: nothing else in the world has the same texture or flavour. It's not even a particularly acquired taste – there is nothing too extreme about it. It is best when bought from a good local butcher in Scotland, but the biggest supplier of good haggis is MacSween's of Edinburgh. They export all over the planet and, if the idea of a sheep's pluck boiled with oatmeal in a stomach lining is too much for you, they also make a vegetarian version. Poached pears and whisky ice cream conclude one of the best meals I've had in around 60,000 miles of travelling.

As we step back out into the street, there is a sense of Brigadoon in the drizzle. It seems improbable that this place could still be there in the daylight of tomorrow. I'm just glad that Masonic architects spared it and saved me from my forlorn fridge.

ANGRY SPICES IN THE AIR - *glasgow*

He's an amateur boxer. A good one. He used to go out with a saucy newsreader. He broke her windows when she broke it off. He was in court about it this morning. He made his money as a oalcsman. Now he owns this restaurant. When he's out of the kitchen, he wears Dolce and Gabbana, dressing like a subplot from *The Sopranos*. His sixty-six-year-old father works for him as a commis. He loves his mum, whose puffy, alcoholic, red face is punctured by two milky evil eyes. He's in the kitchen now, ordering the Russian waitress in the miniskirt to get that jar off that top shelf again. He paces the galley by the hot plate. Testosterone ripples the air like midday heat rising from hot tarmac. He swivels to meet my eye. Well, the top of his paper hat meets my eye.

'Fancy a few rounds in the ring?'

Yes, that's me he's asking: the skinny, slightly effete commis he didn't like from shift one.

'Oh, I love boxing, but I'm afraid I have a rehearsal tonight and, anyway, I like the shape of my nose as it is, thanks.'

He doesn't say anything. He doesn't move. He just stands there and stares at me. I don't move either. I stare back. I think it's called dumb insolence. Or fear. Or not giving a damn. I hate this guy. I hate this job. My weekly wage is less than he'd spend on a garish tie. I am so skint I can't walk out. So I stand there. I imagine taking my Sabatier and ramming it into his temple. I imagine one more week. That's all I need: one more week and I can pay the rent I owe. So I stare. Another ten seconds of silence. I can smell the kebabs burning. I can smell the sharpness of my sweat. I can smell his. They mix like angry spices in the air.

'I'll do it.'

He spins to face the source of the voice. It's James, the kitchen porter. A big guy, sixteen, and six weeks out of school, with a big slow head and a big slow smile, a grey wet towel in his big red hand.

A smirk appears on the boxer like a vicious paper-cut. He walks to James. His head is parallel with his chest. He tips it slowly back.

'Think you can go a few rounds?'

'Well, I've never tried, but it looks like fun.'

He laughs.

'Right! Get changed! Let's go!' He stamps off, electricity in his clogs, then suddenly halts, like a cartoon villain. He looks back at me.

'I'll see you tomorrow.'

He's gone. It's quiet. I turn the kebabs over and head downstairs for a drum of rapeseed oil. Tomorrow I will walk in and see James's mangled nose and blackened eyes. I'll know that if I leave I won't pay my rent. I won't give a damn. When I walk back to my flat, freedom will race like whisky through my veins.

SAVELOY DIP - *south shields*

The North Sea blows up King Street and through my overcoat.
I'm in South Shields, where my grandmother lives, and we're
queueing outside Dickson's Pork Shop, waiting for a saveloy
dip. The tiny shop is a centre of frenetic activity. A gang of ten
women snap 'Next!' with controlled efficiency, sucking us
inside, where we are overwhelmed by steam and the singing
murmur of Geordie gossip. A big-eyed baby in a pushchair
looks up at me, holding a huge sausage like a lollipop in his
fists. I'm asked what I want on my dip. 'Everything, please.'
'Everything' means that the soft roll is spread with strong
mustard, pease pudding and soft sage-and-onion stuffing, to
make a savoury setting for the smoked sausage. Then comes
the dip. An inch and a half of bun sticks out of the paper
wrapper and is dunked into the boiling sausage water. It is
immediate and reassuring, rich and revitalizing. It's hot and in
my hand. I like fast food this way.

It tastes as if it could have come from Hamburg or some other
German city. Indirectly, it did. In the late nineteenth century,
German immigrants settled in the north-east, and in the
process of British naturalization, were transformed from
Schweinmetzgers into pork butchers. My grandparents remember
shops owned by Dietz, Siebe and Dummler families, which
aren't typical Geordie names. During the First and, particularly,
the Second World War, these families were pilloried and bullied,
as jingoism swept the nation. Just as the Battenburgs became
Mountbattens, those that didn't go out of business anglicized
their names. Although the names disappeared, the flavours
remained and became, with fish and chips, the local fast food.

Along with stottie cake, the soft, open-textured bread which looks like a large muffin, pease pudding is one of the reasons I look forward to visiting the north-east. You can get it in cans elsewhere in the country, but it's grey and bland. The best pease pudding is made by filling a muslin bag with yellow split peas, then boiling them beside a leg of ham. As they swell, they are crushed against the bag's sides. The smooth, puréed texture is similar to that of hummus. As a kid, I used to visit my other grandmother in Greece. There wasn't much in common between the grannies' diets, but they both ate pease pudding. The Greek version, fava, is also a form of fast food, but in a different way. It is the staple of the week of fasting that precedes Christmas in the Orthodox Church. The only real difference is that my Geordie grandmother doesn't garnish her pease pudding with garlic and olive oil.

One of my favourite memories from childhood is of eating pease pudding while listening to my granddad tell stories. In the dining room of my grandparents' house, there was a large bevelled mirror above the mantelpiece opposite the table. As he told his tales, he would glance at his reflection, as if to check that he had the right expression for the scene. The stories were always gripping and usually ended in violence: how he still had his milk teeth when he was ten, so asked his friend to knock them out with a block of wood; how he helped his big sister pass clothes through a mangle, until she mangled the little finger of his left hand (cue demonstration of mangled digit); how he lost the tip of the middle finger of his other hand when the pit roof collapsed when he was working as a miner aged fourteen, and the only thing that saved him was the pony by his side which took the weight (cue demonstration of mangled digit); how he was shot as a joiner during the Second World War when a captain didn't notice he was still building the targets for artillery practice and ordered his company to open fire (cue demonstration of entry and exit wounds on tattooed forearm). I still love to eat pease pudding as often as I can because, when I do, I can still hear his voice.

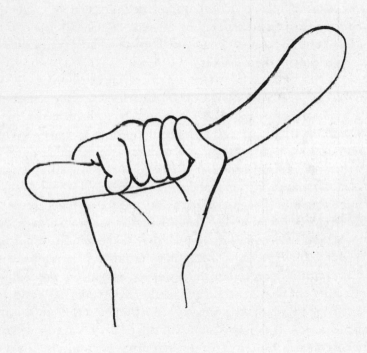

BRACE YOURSELVES - *glasgow*

The birds lie beautiful, iridescent against the folds of a polythene bin bag. They don't look peaceful. They look dead. They're a brace – a young couple. My mind races with macabre romanticism, imagining the dead lovers' characters. He's a preening fop, proud and dandy. She's a Laura Ashley librarian; shy, but bright. Her sensitivity coupled with his sense of unbridled adventure gives them that impenetrable air of invincibility that is exuded by soulmates when confronted by the tedious insignificance of the rest of creation. I don't know whether I should cut their heads off first or pull off their feathers.

The pheasants are a present from my friend Gordon. His dad is a gamekeeper near Loch Lomond who breeds birds in an abandoned anti-aircraft battery at the foot of Queen's View. Guineafowl, peacocks, grouse and rare-breed hens peck for grit and grains amongst rusting MOD miscellanea and abandoned Vespa frames. I decide to take the feathers first and start with him. I keep him in the bin bag to catch his clothes as I strip him. Because he's been hanging for twelve days, he's ripe, and they come off easily. I try to be gentle. When I'm careless, his skin rips, revealing the yellowy fat underneath. His dignity is plucked until he's naked apart from the feathers around his head. He looks like a murdered gangster, humiliated in death, wearing nothing but his trilby and brilliantine. His bumpy skin is bruised a violent purple from where he was shot. I carve the lead from his wounds. His moll takes less time, as if she doesn't care so much about losing her dowdy dress. As I cut off their heads, they are transformed. They are no longer creatures with a personality. They are meat.

I am embarrassingly squeamish. When I see blood and suffering, I faint. When I watched *Dirty Pretty Things* on a flight recently, I passed out during the operation scene and was woken by Nick McCarthy and a steward slapping my face. As I pull the wormy entrails out of the birds, I feel nothing, however. I wonder if it's because I've gutted hundreds of birds before, but it's not. It's because it's no longer a bird. It's now meat, and there's no compassion for meat. It scares me when I consider the implications of this, so I don't. I get on with it. I brown the pieces, put them in a casserole dish with some vegetables and herbs, then drown them with a bottle of wine. A few hours later, there is a general candle-lit murmuring of 'rich', 'tender', 'gamey', etc. Beautiful feathers lie under peelings and coffee grounds, like a secret between a murderer and his dead.

LIKE CHRISTMAS SHOULD BE -*munich*

When I'm on tour, I feel less of a sense of season than I do in real life. It can be any time of year backstage or onstage. To remind myself that it's winter, I wander with my band-mates to the Munich Christkindlmarkt. Under our feet, the sycamore leaves are as clear and dry as the cold air. We cross the tram tracks to the ice rink at the foot of the grand Justizpalast building. Schläger Euro-beat propels Münchners politely clockwise around the ice. Toddlers learn to stay skating upright by pushing a plastic bear on skis.

There's a smell of smoke and spices in the air. Paul, our drummer, dribbles onion sauce from a Schweinenackensteak over his leather gloves. He gives me a bite of a corner and it's good — a pork-chop sandwich with a spicy and intense taste, like boar. I spot an odd couple of middle-aged women warming their hands on paper cones of chestnuts. One has a pink pom-pom that trembles as she laughs; the other is sour-faced in sable collar and cuffs. I grab a cone and crack the chestnuts as we walk towards the Rathaus (the town hall), around which the wooden cabins of the market are clustered. One contains a couple of copper cauldrons brimming with *Glühwein*. Standing in a circle, we sip and blow clouds of cloves and cinnamon at each other and munch on Lebküchen: soft gingerbread cakes sealed in a very thin wafer then dipped in chocolate and icing sugar. It's the same wafer that is used for communion and is wrapped around the cakes to preserve them through the winter.

The stall next door sells *Nüssknäckers*, and among them are the most elaborate nutcrackers I've ever seen. Like Chitty Chitty Bang Bang extras, a platoon of foot-and-a-half-tall wooden soldiers stands to attention with open, toothy mouths. Put a nut between their teeth, yank their arms and they'll spit out the cracked pieces for you. I'm still hungry and find more Munich street delicacies. *Leberkäse* is, literally, 'liver cheese' and looks like a loaf of bread, but is really a baked pâté. A slice is tasty in a roll, covered in sticky, sweet, dark mustard. I follow it with a slab of *Krustanbraten* – pork crackling, that which looks like varnish under a heat gun.

Everything smells and feels like December should. A man with a face pink from the cold hides a smile under a huge, curving moustache. His felt hunter's hat has a twig of mistletoe tucked into the brim. He has a beatific calm about him, as if he knows he has found the purpose of his life: standing in the Christmas cold, blue eyes twinkling as he warms Bavarian bellies with baked apples.

Shall we get a Chinese takeaway? Fish and chips? What about some Italian food? Would you all like pizza? It's 1983, and this is a rare treat as, like most suburban British families, we rarely eat out. We've just moved to Glasgow and, as there is no oven or fridge, we have to look to the outside world for food.

We cruise around the sludgy January streets in a metallic green Morris Marina until we come across an illuminated plastic sign that reads 'Romy's' in an extravagant script. 'PIZZA' is exclaimed in powerful capital bold below. As we drive back, the car is filled with the smell of hot grease, newspaper and vinegar, mingling with the vinyl aroma of the beige seats. The alien scenery of a new city blurs past behind heavy condensation. I'm not interested. I'm hungry and I'm excited. Back on the bare boards of the new house, I sit cross-legged by my brother and unpeel the paper to reveal a golden disc perched on a mound of soft, slippery chips. Because it has been deep-fried, it looks like a huge coin. This is Italian food. I file this in my mental reference library and notice that oil comes out when I squeeze the foam-like bread between my thumb and finger.

A couple of decades later, I'm sitting by my Italian friend Alice in the Trattoria della Pesa, a traditional Milanese restaurant. As each course appears, she explains a little about it. '*Zibello* is named after a small town near Parma. The *culatello* is a fillet that is wrapped in muslin then soaked in white wine before it's cured, which is where the pale-pink colour comes from. *Cappone* is castrated as a young rooster, so the flesh tends to have a more delicate flavour. *Mostardo* are a spicy candied fruit, both sweet and savoury. *Risotto al salto* is dry and, particular to the north, is traditionally reheated from the day before. When we say '*infinocchiare*', we're talking about fennel, but the phrase is also used to mean taking the piss or taking advantage, from when fennel used to be served before wine was tasted at a meal; its anaesthetic properties disguised the bad taste. *Lingue di gatto* are 'cats' tongues', delicate butter biscuits that melt on your tongue.'

Each explanation is novel and exciting, triggering my saliva glands and imagination. I realize how little I know about the regional complexity and nuances of Italian food. There's more to it than deep-fried pizza.

We're on the steps of the cathedral in the old town of San Sebastián. Andy is frowning at a slice of octopus dangling from the point of his cocktail stick. The flesh is unblemished white with a purple-pink tinge around the suckered edge, cut on the diagonal in a graceful oval. People with a drink in one hand and a plate of tapas in the other surround us. They're overspill from Casa Alcalde, a timeless bar decorated with bullfighting posters and hams hanging from the ceiling which drip fat into the paper cones at their base. It's not called tapas here, but *pinxos*, after the cocktail sticks spiked into each of the delicacies on the glass counter: sardines, chorizo, manchego cheese, several shades of cured ham, whitebait, fried cheeses, tomatoes and tiny baby eels. You fill your plate, and then when you're full, the server counts the sticks and charges you.

'Go on. It's just like chicken.'

It's always 'just like chicken': partridge, snake, rabbit, frog's legs, human. Any alien flesh you've never tried before.

On my thirteenth birthday, my mum made tea for a few of my friends. There was a bowl of olives on the table. My dad's Greek, so we ate a lot of Mediterranean food as I grew up. Ewan didn't. His diet was more traditional West Coast of Scotland – Lorne sausage, potato waffles and Angel's Delight. He'd never seen an olive before. That seems odd in 2006, but in Glasgow in 1985, olives were odd.

'What's this?'

'It's an olive.'

'What's that?'

'It's just a thing you eat.'

'What's it taste like?'

At this point my mother came into the room.

'Do you like grapes?'

'Yeah, I love grapes.'

'You'll probably love olives then.'

Of course he didn't. His face contorted as the expected sweetness gave way to the lie of briny bile, revolted mouth twisting to drop a pool of black gob on the plate. I'm still amazed by my mother's reasoning. As Andy starts to chew, I absentmindedly guess at the thought process: Grapes look like olives — I like grapes — I like olives — they taste like each other. There's fear in the eyes.

The revolted mouth twists.

Out it comes.

'It's nothing like chicken.'

AROLA'S KITCHEN - *madrid*

I'm sitting in Sergi Arola's kitchen in La Broche, Madrid. He is wearing a washed-out Blackhawks T-shirt and is joking about how he only started cooking to buy gear for his band. He doesn't mention either of his Michelin stars.

A green-tinted chalkboard on the wall is covered in dense, neat text and diagrams, as if from a physics lecture theatre. It's the menu. Our table is directly in front of the main preparation area. There are sixteen chefs and sixteen serving staff. The restaurant seats thirty-two.

To get us salivating, we are brought bread, oil and three types of salt: olive black, smokey brown and spiced vivid pink. Each tastes more of the flavour of its colour than it does of salt. A thick glass tablet appears with a bonbon of *foie* custard cream and a spot of caramel gleaming like polished amber. It is like a fine Belgian truffle, only savoury. It's an introduction to the baffling sensory overload that will follow with the next ten tiny courses. As a spoonful of chestnut soup with bacon ice cream passes my lips, I want to laugh, because I can't believe what's happening in my mouth. I've never experienced this before. After early childhood, there are few opportunities to experience a completely novel sensation, so when you come across one, you're not quite sure what to do.

The delicate precision of the food is almost incomprehensible. The sardines come smoked with a crispy fried egg. The yolk from a bantam chicken is wrapped in brittle pastry which cracks when tapped. The dexterity required to separate the yolk, and then to wrap and fry it is stunning. Still, the food is not fussy; it's almost rustic. Pork and veal sausage with white beans, Idiazábal cheese risotto: it is as if Spanish rural cooking has been concentrated, refined and reduced to its essence. I've never eaten in a Michelin-starred place before. It's not like normal eating. It's abstract, like listening to a Frank Zappa record – interesting, but when a recognizable tune appears, it's only as an ironic reference.

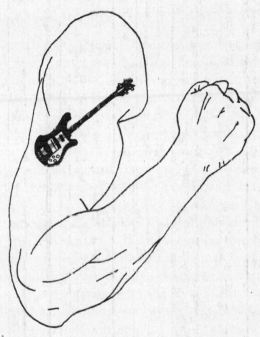

A few hours later, we're backstage after the gig and Sergi's chatting with Bob, a fellow bassist. He rolls up his sleeve and shows off a tattoo of a Rickenbacker. 'Ooh, that's just like mine,' says Bob. I can't imagine Bob rolling back his sleeve to reveal a couple of inky Michelin stars.

A CHRISTMAS CEREMONY - *edinburgh*

The drone drifts down from somewhere sinister in the draughty Victorian terrace. Is it the swelling hum of a swarm of African killer bees? Is it the malevolent crescendo of an approaching squadron of Lancaster bombers? Is it the low chanting of satanic priests in their temple of doom? Or is it the frustrated trumpeting of a rutting bull elephant? No. It's my pal Craigie piping in the pudding.

It's Christmas day, sometime in the early eighties. He is a year younger than me and has been learning the martial art of bagpipes. We're in the festively austere Edinburgh house of his family, who are friends of ours, waiting for the approach of the pudding. His mother made it a year ago, then buried it somewhere secret until yesterday, three hundred and sixty-four days for the spices, dried berries and bevvy to mingle and change their flavours into the richest treat, then steamed in a clootie overnight. This is my density.

This is the highlight of Christmas dinner. Never mind the boring, dry turkey meat, I'm palpitating with anticipation, as the mournful drone heralds the moistened fruit cannonball audibly nearer, the harsh notes flying from his Craigie's chanter like a volley of Bannockburn arrows. The hall is tall and dark, the racket echoing off the floorboards and walls, the shadows chasing the faint blue brandy flames that lick the black, supernatural globe held on a platter by his mother. My brother covers his ears as Craigie and pudding enter the candlelit dining room. The fire cracks angrily, spitting sparks at the hearth. Craigie's wearing his new fawn trousers and his father's tartan tie, his over-inflated face purple with effort as he breathes a gale of life from his straining lungs into the tartan octopus fighting under his arm. His wee sister looks up with large brown eyes, deely-boppers quivering on her head as she chews the same bit of turkey she's had in her mouth for twenty-five minutes.

I take a sip of watery orange squash from a pink Tupperware cup that tastes of plastic. I resent the cup. It's the symbol of my discontent. I'm eight years old! Why the hell are they giving me a plastic cup? Do they think I'd break a glass? I'm not six. The last alcohol flame flickers out.

Craigie and I like to set fire to things. Last Christmas, we found some paraffin in his father's shed and stole his mother's cigarette lighter. We made a bomb and burned off my brother's brows and lashes. How we laughed.

Craigie drops the mouthpiece; a string of saliva stretches like spider silk from his lips. The last note dies. Is this as close to the sound of death that an instrument can get? That final wheeze of reedy wind, like the gasp of a corpse as it's lifted from its deathbed, squeezing the air from the cold lungs. His face deflates to its normal size. The ceremony is over. It is time to eat.

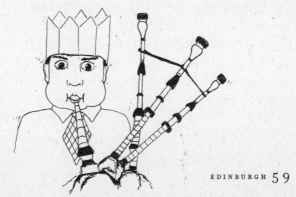

The lampshades on each side of the door of Sean's Panaroma are rusty frying pans. The view is good, but Bondi is overcast and the ocean is grey. The beach looks uncannily like South Shields in early March. Four surfers are out in the drizzle. The restaurant has a good name. If a chef has a sense of humour, the food is likely to be loved.

'We bake our own bread,' says the waitress, presenting a bottle of Nolan's Road olive oil as if it were twenty-year-old claret. The ceremony seems too much until I taste it. It is clear and as drinkable as cold water, but with wheatgrass freshness. Pink flakes of salt from the banks of the Murray River sit on the shell of a Sydney rock oyster. The perforated wooden wall panelling is reminiscent of the BBC Maida Vale studio. Because the bar between the kitchen and the restaurant is mirrored, you can gaze at the ocean, even if you aren't facing the window.

The Western Australian freshwater marron (a large crayfish) arrives pretty on the plate, pinkish-red with puffs of parsley fried a vivid green. It's sweet, between a small lobster and a large langoustine. Equally pretty are the heirloom tomatoes in my friend's salad. Black, yellow and heavy red – some are fleshy and friendly, some tart and bitchy; all are different and stimulating. The Festoni pasta doesn't leap from the chalkboard menu, but as the waitress describes the chilli oil, rocket, Parmesan and lemon, she pauses. 'It's Sean's signature. He's served it every night for twelve years.' You can sense the affection – the sheets of handmade corrugated pasta, tumbled together like tin roofs.

It's always thrilling to discover new combinations of flavours, and astringent rosemary cuts lightly through the sweetness of white chocolate and pistachio nougat which might otherwise have been cloying. Darkness falls and the surf swells, breaking on the beach like white rabbits falling from the curve of a rollercoaster. I leave the Panaroma, glancing up at a patch of unfamiliar stars scattered between the clouds.

'You'll need your bib. It's going to get messy.' A white plastic apron is rolled neatly beside my chopsticks and ceramic bowl. Laid on the linen, gleaming surgically, is a set of chrome instruments — serrated edges, clamping grips and probing forks. Across the laminated menu, rolling red script reads 'Harry's Singapore Chilli Crab Restaurant (Same Gurus Since 1982)'. A tower of flimsy wooden bowls clatters on to the table. 'That's for the debris. There'll be a lot of that.'

I'm eating with the band and some Australian friends. We've been let in on Sydney's secret: primal eating at its best. Entering the restaurant, we pass a stack of plastic crates containing the huge green monsters we are about to devour — freshwater mud crabs from the river estuaries of the Northern Territories near Darwin. I bend over for a closer look and their eyes flick violently as they rear, straining heavy claws against thick blue twine, desperate to rip my nosey nose off. Ten minutes later, their magnificence is shattered and they're coated in barbecue sauce, a jumble of legs and claws roasted red. I fight my obsessive-compulsive fear of stickiness and grab a set of glistening tarantuline legs and set to with the implements. The flesh is sweet — sweeter than their salty pals from the ocean. With each course comes another nest of limbs in a different sauce: pepper and salt; chilli; ginger and shallot; oyster; black bean. One of the debris bowls holds a puddle of murky water. A sliver of lemon floats among the flakes and scum. We dip our fingers and rinse ineffectually before wiping them on scraps of napkin.

It's tasty. It's also fun. The best of eating is the best of social activity. Crunching, cracking, sucking, slurping and laughter surround me. The Aussies babble about barbecues. 'I've just got a Beefmaster.' 'Is that the one with the rôtisserie?' 'No, but it has a wok burner!' 'Yeah, but it's all about the implements.' 'Have you got a Wiltshire Bar B Mate?' 'Too right! Slicing edge, spatula, fork, bottle-opener and sausage-pricker — all on one tool!' My belly's stretched, my tastebuds have been entertained, and I'm surrounded by people I want to be surrounded by. Outside, a green neon sign flashes 'Good Vibe'. I silently agree.

Acland Street in Melbourne is lined with cake shops. The windows are loaded with rum cigars, chocolate tunnels, cherry strudels and florentines. Oversized blue and pink meringues, like vivid dollops of concrete, prick the eyes with their artificial intensity. The end of the street is the end of the line. A three-carriage tram, ornate in muted burgundy, stands at the terminus, loaded with passengers. They sit at starchy linen. Mid-*flambé*, a chef stands looking out at us. Wow! A tram restaurant thing! It moves! My band-mates are excited. We discover that you have to book a month in advance. Excitement fades, grapes sour. I recall the revolving restaurant where I last ate in Atlanta. The view was awfully spectacular, but the food was spectacularly awful. The prawns tasted of fleshy water. I convince myself that riding around Melbourne as if we were on the Orient Express wouldn't be so great after all.

We are in the suburb of St Kilda, where we are recording. Along with Fitzroy, it is the hip area of Melbourne. Overlooking the terminus is the bar and restaurant Bigmouth, a windowed wedge of Deco on the corner. The walls are painted shades of Australian coffee — flat white and short black. Candle flames flicker in orange bevelled glasses. Until the thirties, the Oakrood Tea House stood on the site, where you could take tea in the trees on platforms built between the branches of an oak. Like much of the city, the menu has a strong Greek presence. Saganaki cheese sizzles off the skillet, dribbled with lemon. Like many places in Australia, Bigmouth is neither particularly formal nor expensive, but the ingredients are quality and prepared with imagination. Cubes of pork belly are poached in olive oil, complemented by sweet apple crisps and contrasted against pungent, crumbling blue cheese. The tortellini is handmade and stuffed with chicken and pistachios – subtle flavours and textures, served without ceremony.

I wander back to the studio satisfied but know that, as I put my head on my pillow tonight, I'll be thinking of how good it would have been to ride around Melbourne on a tram, the crockery tinkling as I tucked into my tea.

The bullet train pulls out of Tokyo station. A huddle of fans waves us off to Nagoya with their signed album covers. It's a tradition that they give us gifts, usually brightly flavoured sweets and crunchy MSG snacks. One tiny chomp and waves of chemical psychosis rush through the veins: tear cartoon-wrapping violently, scrabble contents, tip them, cram them. Stuff Your Mouth. Chomp! Chomp! Swallow! 'Save me! I need MORE! *I DON'T EVEN LIKE THEM!*' The sweets stay wrapped. Instead, I pick up the beautiful card game that Maiko, an extra-dedicated fan, handed me. *Toto-Awase*, or Sushi Bar, is like pictorial dominoes and is 'the best way to learn about Japanese food fish culture'. The cards have descriptions such as 'the rosy *isaki* flesh is moderately fat with a deep taste' and 'in winter, *hobo* has the highest fat content and rich flavoured milk-white flesh'.

Bullet trains are different from British trains. The families of the high-stressed, high-powered businessmen who jump in front of them have to pay ¥200,000 for every minute the train is delayed. Apparently. We're travelling at a noiseless 200mph as Paul, our drummer, and I order bento boxes. Eating in Japan is often an adventure. Even if there are pictures to accompany the alien symbols, I'm usually clueless. Paul looks nervous – 'I'm terrified that I'm going to eat something I'll have to spit out.' I'm not so bad. The only thing I ever spat out here was yellow, snot-like, raw sea urchin that gleamed like the

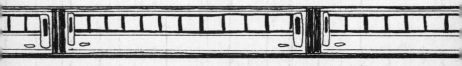

blowings of a heavy head cold. It was involuntary. The muscles in my throat did a weird, rapid contraction and hacked it back out without my permission. It happened quickly and neatly enough for my Japanese companions and me to ignore it and continue the stiff, smiling politeness of the meal undisturbed.

The black plastic box is in compartments. As far as I can make out, the contents are: clams steeped in ginger; unidentifiable fruit or vegetable spicy pickle; mushy chicken ball; barrel-shaped root vegetable; black mushroom; an omelette tied in a knot; crispy fish skin; chewy crab sausage; not sure, maybe fermented entrails; rice; salty plum. I wash the fascinating flavours down with Shizuoka green tea. Paul has a bottle of Pocari Sweat – a 'healthy beverage that smoothly supply the lost water and electrolytes from perspiration. With appropriate density and electrolyte fluid that is close to that of human body fluid, it can be absorbed into the body.' There are a lot of unusual drinks available in Japan, usually from vending machines. The word 'Sweat' doesn't have the unsavoury connotations it may have to Westerners – in Japan, sweating is regarded as noble, the product of work. Pocari Sweat is what you drink to return what you have lost from your body. Still, the salty-sweet, cloudy liquid does look like a bottle of it.

The train pulls into Nagoya. A huddle of fans wave their unsigned album covers and sweets in greeting.

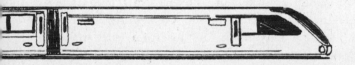

I am eating in Osaka and entrust myself entirely to the perfect taste shown by my Japanese hosts. Akiko and Fukima translate the menu — symbols painted on teak tickets that hang from brass pins on a board. Smelt, sashimi, *fugu*. *Fugu?* Isn't that blowfish? Excitement yelps around the table. Fear chases it, propelled by vague and venomous statistics like poisonous humming birds eager to spear any sense of adventurousness. One in a hundred servings is fatal, don't you know? The order is made.

The sashimi is, as always, beautiful, like slices of semi-precious stone resting on a snowdrift of shredded *daikon* radish. It is from the surface end of the root, so is mild and refreshing. The thin tip is the hot end. Before we put the fish in our mouths, we wrap it in *shiso*, a light, lemony herb that looks a little like nettle leaves and which I have seen only in Japan. I barely notice that I now use my chopsticks with ease rather than the unnatural rigidity of a child holding a pencil for the first time. There is a token Western dish. It is not a standard Caesar salad; shredded kos is topped with fried potato noodles, raw salmon and a barely poached cold egg. The *iwatani* flame is lit below the *nabe*, a pot of cabbage, bean sprouts and fatty beef, raw like bacon.

The idea of food as entertainment is very important in Japan. The first time we visited, the girls from the record label took us, jet-lagged, to a place called Ninja. It was a themed adventure. When I walked in, the girl at the bookings desk brusquely ordered me back outside. 'Your ninja not ready yet! Outside!' I stood sheepishly in the street with the others, watching the blocks of lucky salt by the doorway dissolve in the warm mist. '*Hai!* Come now! Ninja ready!' We clattered back down the stairs. 'Ninja! Ninja!' she cried, then clapped her hands twice. Another girl burst from a secret door into a forward roll in front of us. She was dressed in black with a scarf around her head. She wasn't an out-of-work actress: she was a ninja. 'Follow me! Watch head!' We followed her through another secret door into a dark passage. It was lit with a low, green light. We stopped by an artificial fountain built into the wall, with plastic plants surrounding it. 'This ninja shrine!' We murmured appropriate awe and agreement. It reminded me of the boat trip you can go on in Blackpool, where you go for a journey around the world, seeing what a guy from Blackpool's idea of Egypt and Africa is. 'Watch head!' We followed her

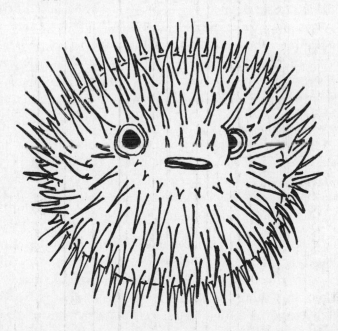

further along the dark passage, abruptly stopping by two windows with bars over them. We looked through and could see more plastic plants and fake rocks. 'This ninja nest!' We murmured appropriate awe and agreement. 'Watch head!' We followed her still further down the passage. We turned a corner. The ninja's face creased in dismay. 'Oh, no! Not ready! Go back!' We shuffled back round the corner. The ninja disappeared. Then reappeared. 'Right! Come now!!' We shuffled after her. 'Oh, no! What happened?' I wasn't sure. She was pointing at the floor in front of us. There was now a sheet of Perspex over some more fake rocks and plastic plants with dry ice curling between them. 'Oh, no! How we get cross?' We murmured appropriate perplexed anxiety. 'It's OK! I'm ninja! *Hai!!*' She clapped twice, and a drawbridge fell down, allowing us to cross the thick Perspex in safety, into the restaurant beyond, where we ate smoke salad and were entertained by another ninja who knew card tricks. Now, a year later, we watch our grinning bassist as he stirs the bubbling mix, chattering about his technique.

Shishamo are small smelt fried whole, their swollen, pregnant bodies twisted with the heat. A bite reveals the eggs; pale yellow, densely packed and so small they look like powder, but they taste of delicious bitterness. Fukima tells me that her parents made her eat lots of *shishamo* as a child, so the calcium in the fragile bones would make her legs grow long.

Finally, the *fugu* is set down to hushed anticipation. I pick up a breaded, deep-fried cube. I chew. I swallow. It tastes good, but not as exceptional as it should, considering the supposed risk in eating it. Findus and Bird's Eye make something similar. What price death? A finger from the Captain's table?

IT'S A FORTUNE - *hong kong*

I turn on the Hong Kong hotel-room TV and it flashes a warning that it is now illegal to keep backyard poultry. Through the window, I can see two lovebirds in a cage hanging from a rusting air-conditioning unit. The bird-flu cull has savaged Hong Kong and the famous Bird Street market is apparently desolate. Still, as I leave the Starck white perfection of the JIA hotel, I wander past the rain-heavy awnings of market stalls where rows of red and yellow ducks hang upside-down, sweet, viscous drops dripping off their bills. A plastic sign flashes 'Chicks'. There's a cartoon of a little yellow chick in case you weren't sure which type of chick was available. One stall sells forty varieties of cabbage, from miniature bok-choi to great wrinkled leaves which flap like elephant ears. Above a butcher's block, bevelled by a billion hits of the cleaver, hang ears and snouts, like morbid masks. I ask what the expensive brown mounds in fancy presentation boxes are, and the answer involves a lot of good health and possibly the tail of a deer. Dozens of hundred-year-old eggs sit caked in black saltpetre. A man with a thousand-year-old face is weighing a plastic carrier bag of squirming shrimp using a four-thousand-year-old technique: the bag hangs off one end of a pivoted stick, and he slides a weight along the other until the stick is horizontal. Water cascades down stepped polystyrene boxes where thirty varieties of fish flap breathlessly, as if death dancing back to their spawning grounds. A tiny woman grabs one and pushes it towards my face, pulling back the gills to reveal their blood-red freshness. A pretty-as-a-doll child laughs as her mother pulls a thrashing, mottled crab from its tank by the grass knots restraining its claws. I turn on to what has to be Puppy Street, as every window is covered in puppy slobber, the puppies bounding fluffily in their allotted four square feet of Perspex cell.

Dusk descends, so we take a taxi to the Temple Street night market, renowned for its street food. There are yellow, tasty-looking tentacles on sticks and dough balls frying, but we are wary of eating suspicious-looking street food on tour after a bowel-dweller which one of our touring party picked up eating on the street in Mexico city. A bowel-dweller which was pulled from its darkened cave in the toilet of a tour bus like a stringy serpent from its lair. Bob distracts me with fortune-tellers. I've never had my fortune told before. I've never wanted to know the excitement or nastiness which may be on its way. This fella has dyed hair and laminated photographs surrounding him of him reading the palms of various dignitaries, celebrities, etc. A notice trumpets that he has appeared on the British BBC. He does Bob first. His life-line is strong – he'll live to his healthy late eighties – but his love-line meanders a little. He has a good business chin and a lucky gap between his teeth. Then there's a lot of boring stuff about saving and spending money in his forties. The fortune-teller takes my hand.

'Life-line strong and deep, but with big break in middle. You going to have nasty accident when thirty-four. Might not survive. No drive car fast or ride in plane.'

It's my thirty-fourth birthday in two weeks. I 'ride in plane' every other day. Is this freak trying to freak me out? He mumbles some irrelevant toss about how to spend money in my forties. I don't notice if he says I have lucky teeth. I'm going to die in two weeks. I may as well eat the yellow tentacles.

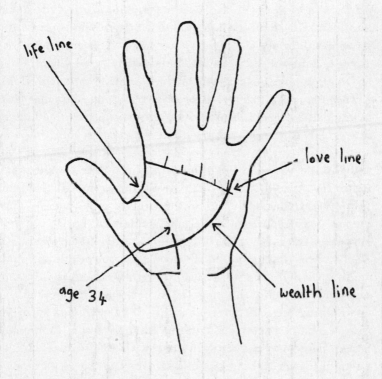

life line

love line

age 34

wealth line

I don't know what day of the week it is. Arab Street of Singapore is closed and shuttered. It's Friday. I celebrate my stupidity with a Thai coconut bought from a guy by Bugis station. With a machete crack, he scalps the fawn shell and drops in a straw. I sip the sweetness, cool against the dense humidity. The smell from the Victoria Street Wholesale Centre envelops the nose like a fusty mattress. A skinny man with silver headphones tosses thousands of tiny dried silver fish in an open-weave basket, white dust coating his flip-flops. Chinese sausages hang translucent in oily finger bunches from bright twine. Hardened bright orange shrimp are piled high by blackened sea cucumbers dried like turds in the sun.

Outside the Va Voom Vietnam Café, the waiter is asleep at a table. Turning on to Liang Seah Street, I pass the Yuk Kee Duck shop. Vivid lilac baby aubergines catch my eye from Nasi Lemak, a Singapore buffet. I take a selection back to a quiet corner of the lobby of the Intercontinental hotel where I'm staying. The violet *brinjal* is delicious, but the real highlight is *otah*, a paste of coconut, chilli and fish wrapped in a banana leaf and roasted. The heat is sweet, but the best bit is unwrapping the leaf. There is a side of *kang hong*, a spinach-like vegetable stir-fried with the shrimp I saw in Victoria Street. They are pungent, intense with the texture of Rice Krispies. Silver fish are sprinkled over the top as a crunchy, salty condiment.

I'm engrossed in stimulating new flavours when an apoplectic face bounces up like a pompous red balloon. Boiled eyes peer down a sneering nose. A lip curls in open contempt. 'Do you mind not eating in MY lobby?' I don't like snobs. 'Do you know who I AM?' I don't like boors. 'I'm the General Manager!' I don't like bullies. I feel embarrassed and mildly humiliated.

Three hours later, when I'm onstage, I invite the six thousand audience members to the hotel for a party. 'Bring some fast food with you.'

When the mob arrives clutching greasy cartons and trampling crumbs into the deep-pile, they transform the lobby into a much happier place. It was such a puerile thing to do, but it turned out to be quite fun. There was a lot of chaos, but it was good humoured.

Revenge is a dish best served not cold, but fast.

Brown stickiness drips over the edge of the cone on to my fingers. I need both hands to hold it. Behind me is a boring statue. Boring old buildings are all around. The boring road is bright white marble, unbearably hot under my sandals, searing coloured flash scars on to my eyes that dance when I close my lids ... I'm five, in Ephesus. My parents want to educate me. I'm not interested. I've never tasted ice cream like this before. Not only does it taste of chocolate, but there are bits of chocolate in it too.

Now, it's a yellow stickiness that drips over the edge. I catch it with my tongue before it hits my fingers and instantly remember Ephesus. Jesus stretches his arms into the haze. Sugar Loaf looms towards me. Copacabana curls below. Rio. By the sea-oh. I've never tasted ice cream like this before. Not only does it taste of sweetcorn, but there are bits of sweetcorn in it: chewy flecks of skin in the deep-yellow ice. Vultures sweep silent arcs beneath the cable car.

Cardboard discs by our plates indicate whether we want more

or not. On the red side, a fat-faced pig pats his bulging belly, hand up in happy resignation: *Não obrigado!* On the green side, he holds his knife and fork, grinning with gluttonous glee: *Sim por favor!* Our Brazilian friends have taken us to the Porcão barbecue restaurant. 'Porcão' means 'big fat pig'. We load our plates with artichoke, palm hearts and mushrooms from an extravagant salad bar. Eduardo's plate is empty. He smiles patiently. Black-aproned waiters emerge through wrought-iron gates from the furnace. Each holds a bayonet of meat, fresh from the flame: sausage, silverside, leg of lamb. Eduardo's disc remains red. A bayonet of picanha appears. The noble cut. The sirloin tip. Eduardo flips to green. The waiter's sabre slices the caramelized outer layer, revealing deep-red moistness. I pick a slice with the tweezers by my plate. It's good. Marta sneers at the idea of filet mignon – soft, but no flavour. A rapier point thuds into the table. What looks like fifty plump cashews are speared on the blade. They are chicken hearts. A dozen are flicked on my plate. They're chewy, extremely rich and meatier than chicken. I hear a murmuring about how Brazilian beef can be eaten by vegetarians, as it is so pure, so organic. The last disc flips from green to red.

NÃO OBRIGADO
NO THANKS

If the stallholders from the duff end of Portobello Road set up in Borough Market, it would feel similar to St Elmo market in Buenos Aires. Its Victorian grandeur is crumbling, the marble counters cracked and stained, the flow of fresh produce clogged by dusty bric-a-brac, like effluent silting up a river. Diego points to a stall and tells me that when he was a kid and came here with his mother, there would be fifty crates of live chickens. She would choose one and – constricted gurgling accompanied by finger across throat – it would be ready to take home. The chickens have gone and, although there are a few greengrocers and butchers left, they occupy a tiny ghetto among the old telephones, stuffed cats, broken toys and used mate gourds. *Yerba mate* is the national drink. You can get it in cafés, but most people drink it from their own gourds, often taking a flask of hot water with them to make it up. It is drunk through a rigid silver straw with a bulbous perforated end that sits in the gourd. The drink is a stimulant and, like caffeine, if you drink enough of it, will make you a wee bit jittery.

Buenos Aires feels more European than anywhere else in South America. The crumbling grandeur is similar to Lisbon or some grimier parts of Paris. The area around Dorrego Square is touristy, but Bar Dorrego on the corner is worth visiting. The rolling art nouveau swirls of the wooden bar and furniture have been whittled away by a century of penknife graffiti. Tangos play on the radiogram and eighty-year-old Bols bottles sit on the shelves. The ham sandwiches are crude blocks of strong, simple flavour.

'*Todo bicho que camina va a parar al asador.*' Anything that walks ends up on the grill. It is a euphemism that summarizes an

Argentinian attitude to culinary and sexual encounters: I have no preference, as long as it's meat.

La Brigada is opposite the market. The menu is bound in hairy hide, branded 'LB'. Drawings of cattle border the page. From shelves slightly above the diners' head height, model bulls peer down on the plates. The napkins are embroidered with horns. There is a theme. We start with empanadas: similar to a Gregg's Steak Bake but with rich, short pastry and beef filling that has been cooked for a minimum of hours. Other than bitter greens and a few chips, there are no vegetables. The waiter brings sweetbreads, wild boar sausage and a selection of beef cuts. He slices with a spoon. Blood leaks in pools on the plate. It rushes to my head. I'm giddy and elated. I won't eat meat again for a month. Not after the last course. *Criadilla*. Mountain oysters. Bull testes. Before they come, I try to imagine what they'll look like. I reckon they'll be at least the size of a lemon. I'm surprised when they're not much bigger than my own. We ask the waiter if he likes them. He sniggers. 'No.' I pierce one with my fork. Clear liquid seeps from the pricks with a spunky stink. I cut off a quarter. Pop it in. Chew. It tastes like a bag of green pennies. It's not good. An ex-girlfriend once objected to the aftertaste of oral sex as being like chewing a bag of green pennies. As that peculiar metallic taste stains my tongue, her pained and twisted face appears, mouthing, 'I told you so.' Everything that walks may end up on the grill, but that doesn't mean you should eat its balls.

DONUTS - *greenpoint*

'You dumb donut-eatin' cop!' Officer Constantine cuffs Officer Kuchner playfully on the back of the head. Kuchner is flirting in Polish with the girl behind the counter of the Peter Pan Donut and Pastry Shop on Manhattan Boulevard, Greenpoint, Brooklyn. She wears a green A-line dress with pastel-pink cuffs and collar. Heavy lashes flicker over her eyes. Constantine is tall. Cheekbones strike boldly from a proud, handsome African-American face. He takes his cap off. A photo of his mother is under the cracked plastic label inside. It is shift change at the 94th precinct on Messerole around the corner. I order an Old-Fashioned and a coffee: $1.70. Officers Sanchez and Suarez show each other pictures of their kids. Heavy flashlights and dull metal pistols hang from their belts. Constantine feels neglected. 'I'm gonna quit my job!'

The other cops glance up.

'I'm gonna be a model!'

'Don't quit too soon,' snaps Pantaleon.

'Look at this face!'

No response.

'I could model underwear!'

Nothing.

'Man, I need to get me a *Do*nut!'

The lashy waitress fills my cup. It is identical to eight million others in delis across the city: blue with a Grecian urn on the side and 'We Are Happy To Serve You' written in Hellenic script That's not always true. She likes my accent. I like hers more — Polish/Brooklyn vowels singing the unknown. Green plastic letters punctuated by shamrocks announce St Patrick's Day. 'To Insure Freshness All Our Products Are Baked On The Premises.' Suffocating the ventilation grill, stringy dust hangs like a sheepskin rug from the lowered ceiling. A guy with a white moustache is complaining that he wanted a jelly donut, not a ring. Lashy points to the purple injection hole. A stunned jaw drops from a white moustache. 'Hey ... Something new! Jelly in a ring!' He bites. 'That's good. That is good!' He gives his wife a sugar-dusted-moustache kiss. She grimaces, but her eyes are happy as she squeezes his arm.

Fifties-cookbook Technicolors pulsate from the stacked glazes. Greens, yellows, pinks, hundreds and thousands like interference in the cathode rays. I bite off a chunk of Old Fashioned, suck coffee into my stuffed mouth. The dough is fluffy and sweet. The surface is crisp, crinkly and undusted. These cops aren't dumb. These are the best donuts in New York.

'I didn't get that poetry reading.' ... 'What's with that?' ... 'We sat around all day and smoked weed.' ... 'I think it cost her sixty, but now she rents it out.' ... 'Have you heard the Noisettes? From England. She's like a black Karen O. Runs around the stage barefoot. No songs. They're super cool. I saw James Murphy in the back room ...'

This is Dumont on Union, Williamsburg: too cheap for how good the food is. It's Sunday breakfast. The waiter checks me out through the amber Perspex of his BluBlocker shades. He has a cartoon sailor tattooed on his forearm. His tight, striped T-shirt doesn't meet his hipster jeans, leaving the firm curve of his pale potbelly naked like a hairy football.

'Yesssss?' he hisses through his moustache.

'Huevos Rancheros, please.'

The best thing about American breakfast is the bacon: thin strips of brittle, salty crunch that shame the watery, pink British rashers from a greasy spoon with their texture of car-door-seal. The coffee doesn't stop, and the juice is fresh from the orange, not the carton. I still find it exotic to wake up, then eat black beans, egg tortillas and guacamole. What guacamole, too – perfect in texture, taste. Everything seems to be perfect: the rickety tables, the best ingredients, the way the food sits on the plate as if it's excited to be there. Williamsburg attracts the exotic, the creative and the annoying. No one sitting around me looks ordinary. They are either good-looking or interestingly ugly. Two guys in the window booth sip Bloody Marys with wilful louche, a longhaired advert for whatever band they're in

or imagine they're in. The girl beside me with bangs and bunches munches a Gruyèrecheeseburger and has 'Hell Yeah' inked across her bicep. The text is slightly too big, as if aware of being there. A man folds a baby-stroller. His piercings rattle as he sits. A woman steps through the velvet curtains across the door to the street wearing an orange Chanel jacket that looks like it belongs in the MoMa exhibition. Elvis sings he's 'All Shook Up'. The mirrors are dull like weathered lead, reflecting the hip and young in the room as if they were forgotten ghosts. Bare pipes still hold an inch of dust from before this was a diner and before Williamsburg lived like this. I look up, and the pressed-tin roof ripples, the features softened by a century of paint and building shift, a huge tapioca skin ready to fall and tastefully smother the diners below.

20 March. It's my thirty-fourth birthday. For a treat, I have gone to Les Halles, Anthony Bourdain's patch of Paris in Manhattan. I have wanted to go for six years, since I read *Kitchen Confidential* when I was working as a chef. I loved how he captured the parallels of rock 'n' roll debauchery in the back kitchen and back stage. I have come for his Rossini: the most decadent burger in NYC. Ground and charred to order, topped with a tranche of homemade *foie gras* and a reduction-of-red-wine-and-black-truffle sauce to dip it into. When I read Bourdain's book, I, like most commis chefs, couldn't afford to eat the food I sent out every night. Now, I'm ordering this delicious opulence seasoned with cruelty. Do I feel guilty? Do I feel sorry for the commis behind the net-curtained kitchen window? Am I glad to, temporarily, not be skint? Do I question my personal morals?

I think about my fifth birthday. I think about the cake, a glorious creation of my mother's, the centrepiece of the feast in the front room of our Sunderland semi. It must have been a Saturday, as I can hear the Roker Park roar in the background as I wait with unsuppressible excitement for the guests to arrive. I have crept in among the balloons, streamers, wrapped parcels and tailless donkey. I evaluate the banquet. Sausage rolls – horrible. Crisps – nice. Sandwiches – horrible. Fizzy drink – nice. Cake – amazing! It's so blue! That is the best colour ever! That's why it's my favourite. The icing is so heavy it looks like there is no cake, just icing. I like this. In yellow piping there is a fat '5'. I WANT IT NOW! I notice my finger. I can't control it. It pokes into the lower curl of the number. It prods and scoops yellow into my mouth. Wonderful sensation of joy rushing happiness to the brain. More probing. More delight. It looks less like a five. There's a fleeting slice of ice and moral dilemma: fear of the SMACK. Logic leads me. If there's no five on the cake, no one will know anything's wrong. I finish the yellow, leaving a smudged sea of blank blue.

I don't remember the consequences. I just remember how good the icing tasted. The burger tasted great too, by the way.

HABITS - *grand canyon*

I wake to the smell of my band-mates' farts. We live on a bus. We're travelling from LA to Tucson and have stopped at the Grand Canyon. The Bright Angel Lodge is made of logs stacked on the edge. 'Are the portions big?' I ask. We're in America. It's a stupid question. 'Everything's as big as the canyon.'

Kelly Clarkson is on the radio. Our pints of mud-brown Colorado Fat Tyre taste of Cadbury's chocolate and smell of Kraft cheese. Everyone is moaning about dry throats from the ubiquitous air conditioning. A flight attendant suggested to Andy that he hang a wet towel over the back of a chair. 'It was sopping wet when I hung it up, bone dry in the morning.' Paul reckons he wouldn't be able to sleep for wondering whether it was dry yet. Then he yells. Boiling cream cheese from a deep-fried jalapeno has landed on his lap.

I eat with these guys every day. Their eating habits are as familiar as the songs we play at night. Paul always covers his plate with a napkin when he's had enough. It's as if he's laying a sheet over a half-eaten corpse. Nick is oblivious to waiters. They stand at his elbow until somebody nudges him to point them out. He then looks startled, as if waking from a coma; confused to find himself in a restaurant. Whenever Bob takes a drink, he has to push his upper lip back from his teeth with the rim of the glass. He shakes his fork between bites. Eating also involves triangles in some way, but I've never quite worked out how. Andy tends to stare at his plate, grey with anxiety, worrying about how the foreign stuff will poison him this time. Apparently, I chew too much and frown when I'm enjoying food.

When New Order toured, Bernard Sumner wanted to kill Peter Hook because of the way he licked his fingers after eating a packet of crisps. None of our habits seem that annoying. Yet. We've only been touring for two and a half years.

I used to share a flat with Nick and Paul, and I used to work with Bob. I knew most of their habits before we stepped on a bus together. Being on the road brings you very close together. It's odd for me now to wake up when I'm home and not hear them through the curtains of my bunk.

My Wrangler's Chilli is rigid with salt in a novelty bowl hollowed out from a bread bun. Dire Straits' 'Walk of Life' is on the radio. Bob pushes his lip back. Paul reaches for his napkin. Andy stares at his plate. Nick doesn't notice the waiter. I don't frown.

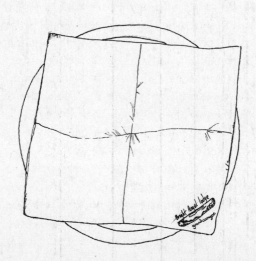

BENTON HARBOR BLUES - *benton harbor*

There's a wok full of pasta tubes glistening green on the stove. Jessica is cooking tonight. Her husband, Bill, is rewiring a ten-channel Flickinger pre-amp into Sly Stone's old mixing desk. Sly's old roaches still lie among the circuitry. Bill and Jessica own the Key Club Studio in Benton Harbor, Michigan, where we are recording for a few days.

I can't work out what's in the sauce that makes it taste so good. Jessica says that she just heated up some cloves of garlic in oil and then mixed in the pasta with mashed avocado: 'It's an easy vegan version of macaroni cheese.' Until recently, Jessica ate only raw foods. All of her allergies disappeared, but it's a hard diet to maintain. Avoiding refined sugar seems to make the biggest difference. She tells me a story about a friend who worked in a Twinkie factory. Staff were forbidden to eat anything from the shop floor. One hungover morning her friend ate one anyway. She woke up in the emergency ward. Apparently, the chemical preservatives that give them a shelf life of more than a year are a little too volatile for human consumption before they're sealed in the wrapper. Twinkies need time to mature.

The other delicacy we had in Benton Harbor was barbecued rib tips, which are gristly cuts of meat served on a couple of slices of white cut loaf and drowned in artificial, sweet sauce that tastes good in a chemically addictive way.

Benton Harbor is almost a ghost town. The buildings that are still occupied creak with neglect in the wind. The shipping industry on which the town's wealth was built collapsed when the interstate freeways were constructed and goods were no

longer transported via the Great Lakes or the Mississippi. It seems an unlikely birthplace for health foods and vegetarianism. At the turn of the twentieth century, the House of David was founded here. It was a gentle religious community which promoted the vegetarian diet and an alternative lifestyle. The men didn't shave or cut their hair. Their baseball team was legendary. The hairies running across the pitch were a popular spectacle. They had their own honey farm and a natural spring, and they invented the sugar waffle cone for ice cream. Allegations of fraud and sexual misconduct against the sect founder cleaved their utopia in the late twenties and, as sexual relations were forbidden, their numbers have dwindled to almost nothing.

It's now 7.30 a.m. I've been awake for twenty-four hours. As I lurch towards the couch, where I will pass out in a few seconds, I notice a few tubes of pasta are still left in the wok.

CAPITOL OYSTERS - *washington dc*

After a show, food options can be grim. A lucky leftover pizza slice or dressing-room scraps — ham that's cracked and hardened from the air conditioning but pink and slippery where the slices overlap. Or Subway. The smell of stale Subway is part of the subtle odour combination that makes the stench of a band's touring van. We're in Washington DC, and I'm not hoping for much, when I get a text message from Nick. 'Ebbitt's Grill. Oysters and Guinness.' It's on the other side of the White House lawn. Floodlit cherry blossom wafts delicate scent over the black railings and ram-resistant concrete blocks. Cops lay placid hands on holstered hips, leaning against a polished patrol car, chatting. It's a surreally peaceful spring night in the capital. The barman is a Scot. Nick is excited because his Westcott Bay oysters were half price. Oysters on special offer? My stomach cramps in warning.

I spy the barman. Grey flat-top and Dickensian specs. High-waisted black apron. Starched white shirt. He left Irvine in 1982 but didn't forget his accent. I wonder if he is going to be a Jimmy MacJimmy. Every town in the world has a Jimmy MacJimmy — an expat parody of a Scot. Although they have not been home in thirty years, their identity is based around being a 'Jock'. Nobody who stays in Scotland describes themselves as 'Jocks'. Jimmies speak with a comical brogue like actors in Disney films about Brigadoon O'Doon or Greyfriar's Bobby. The vocabulary is archaic. 'Acccchhh — they muckle jooabbies urrr braaaaw!' When they learn you are from Glasgow, they lean a wee bit too far into your face.

There's a Jimmy MacJimmy in Manhattan, who runs a fish and chip shop. When we were shooting the video for the song 'Do

You Want To?', we wanted some chips as a prop. We didn't want *fries*, those lightweight twigs the unfortunate many in the rest of the world have to eat, but *chips*. Thick, soggy wedges of greasy potato like you can only get at home. Or Manhattan. You can get anything in Manhattan. Any flavour from anywhere on the planet is there, including real chips. So the runner brought the hot paper parcels back and Jimmy followed, the smell of Scotland in his nostrils and the smell of whisky on his breath. He stumbled around the set searching for us, shaking our hands and crushing them with grievous bodily enthusiasm. The more famous you are, it seems the more people want to squash the bones in your fingers when they meet you. I'm not very famous. It must be tough on the digits of David Bowie. Or Lou Reed – his handshake is barely there – a whisper of palm against palm. A German journalist told me that he interviewed him once and was told by his press officer not to offer to shake his hand, as he had injured it. The interview went well, both warming to each other. As he got up to leave, Reed offered his hand to shake. The journo was baffled, so Lou explained that he got the press officer to tell the injury story. People are intimidated when they meet him, so they tend to bone-crush to show that they aren't. It's easier for him to avoid shaking this way than to explain why he won't shake.

Ryan is all right, though. He knows everything about Rangers and oysters. He tells me I should try a couple of dozen Olympias from Washington State. Tiny and intense — grey pearls shivering on thumbnail shells. DC is a city of extremes: Anglo-Saxon affluence and African-American poverty. Ebbitt's is a bastion of the former. Built in the mid-nineteenth century, the bar was, and is, a hangout of the political elite. Glass cases are stocked with antique shotguns and a wooden flock of decoy ducks. An oil-painted rusty gundog leaps from a frozen lake. The carved mahogany booths are cushioned in velvet. I scrape the shells and listen to Ryan talk about the days of Gazza's glory. It's so very lonely when you're two thousand light-years from home.

SCHWARTZ'S BIFTEK - *montreal*

Schwartz's Charcuterie Hebraïque de Montreal is on St
Laurent near St Cuthbert, opposite M. Berson's yard of granite
gravestones. The rained-on queue is long, stationary and
patient. There are other Hebrew delicatessens within yards,
but they are all empty. Short-order chefs stand bored by their
broilers. They don't have The Legend. Schwartz's has been
smoking its meat daily since 1930. The *viande fumée* is an
institution: one of the reasons why Montreal is Montreal.

The restaurant is strip-light bright and busy. Parker and I
squeeze on to a table of adolescent boys in tracksuits. Their
conversation is a search for opportunities to accuse each other
of being gay. The walls are tiled in white, the floor in cracked
terracotta. It looks like it is swept only at the end of the night,
so as not to disturb the decorative debris of skid-mark fries
and meaty crumbs. We're sitting by the open charcoal broiler –
a prehistoric monster of a machine with whitening ash and
cast-iron bars under a crooked chimney vent. Four slices of
liver sizzle angrily as the chef drops them on the bars. The
walls are papered with newspaper cuttings and signed photos
of stars that like to eat there – Tina Turner, Shania Twain and
the Ink Spots. There isn't a typical customer. An older couple
mutter in Quebec French as if continuing a thirty-year
argument. A woman in a tweed showjumping jacket sits beside
a crusty in combats. There are a few families and a biker in a
yellow Harley T-shirt who passes forkfuls of meat through the
fronds of a moustache which droops over his moving mouth
like two mangy grey otters kissing. There are six choices on the
menu that are mainly different ways of serving *viande fumée* –
as a sandwich, with fries, as part of a combo platter, as part of
a special combo platter. We order *viande fumée*. It's similar to

the salt beef in a Brick Lane bagel. We're each given a plate of the dark-pink-marbled slices, half a loaf of cut white bread, mayonnaise-free coleslaw and a tube of mustard. We follow the example of our neighbours and make sandwiches. The boys are boisterous and awkward, braying at each other with brash insecurity. The biggest one accusingly yells that he has run out of bread. Parker offers him some of his. He seems surprised and thanks him. There's an eruption of scornful laughter, like pus exploding from an overloaded pimple.

'Enjoy your mooched bread!'

'Moocher!'

'Dumbass!'

Moocher deflects the abuse by hacking up and gobbing on his fat cornichon pickle. He meets the eye of the main alpha wannabe.

'Bet you can't eat this pickle, gay boy.'

Spittle dribbles from the ridged tip. Without wavering, gay boy puts it in his mouth.
Clamps teeth.

Halves it.

Silence.

He's the man now.

I can't work out where the food is from. Maybe the Middle East? There's yoghurt, parsley, lentils and lemon on the menu, but also a long list of vodkas. Maybe Ukrainian? Georgian? Inside, a couple are rubbing their bellies like cartoon cats who have snacked on a mouse. They beckon me in with vigorous waves. I may as well go. I have been walking along Queen Street, Toronto, and I am hungry. I have come from the Done Right Inn, a homely dive bar with the Dead Kennedies on the jukebox. The beaten sofas would have been a great Sunday refuge, but they ran out of food. I walk into Banu and feel I have crashed a party only to discover that I was a guest all along.

'Come in! Have a seat! It's our first day!' It is their first day of business. 'Do we look nice? What do you think? You didn't know the type of food? It's Persian!' I love Iranian food. It is delicate and exciting. My Aunt Soori and my friend Andrew's mother cooked it for me when I was a kid. They both left Iran after the revolution, as did the siblings who run Banu, when they were toddlers.

I feel like a seventeenth-century spice trader at a desert feast as they bring me home-squeezed pomegranate juice, yoghurt sprinkled with rose petals, aubergine paste with whey and walnuts and *shashlik* lamb wrapped in thin *lawasa* bread with fresh mint and basil leaves. I ask Samarin, one of Banu's owners, about the vodka. 'It was the main drink before the revolution. At truck stops, the drivers would stop for a couple of shots and a kebab. We're trying to re-create the cosmopolitanism of our country in the seventies.' Samarin is petite, fizzing with gentle energy. Her shirt reads: 'Rosa Parks:

Tehran Needs You! For I Am Also Jim Crowed.' 'It's apartheid

ROSA PARKS: TEHRAN NEEDS YOU! FOR I AM ALSO JIMCROWED

for women. I went back in 1999 and couldn't stand strangers telling me to cover myself. Iran used to be such a progressive society.' There is a flash of pride in her eyes. 'There's still a huge counter-culture — 70 per cent of the population is under thirty, but they see politics as dirty. Bush is a retard. Without him, there would be no Ahmadinejad.'

The back of her shirt reads 'love' in Farsi. There is a lot of love in Banu: love of food and love of a lost home. I leave satisfied, full of food and hope for Samarin and her brothers and sisters.

The beat of the World's Most Dangerous Polka Band bursts
through the swing doors of the Polka Lounge. Lu Sneider takes
her place at the piano. She's played every evening of the forty
years that Nye's Polonaise Room, Minneapolis, has been open.
She knows more than five hundred songs, and anyone can sing
along with her if they feel up for it. A couple of Polish
granddads in anoraks join her. They beam beatifically as they
wail and wander through a tune. It may be 'Delilah'. Red swirls
of carpet flow wall-to-wall like molten lava. The furniture is
vinyl Chesterfield — gold sparkle booths and burgundy wing-
backed bar stools. Most of the waiting staff are over fifty and
wear black bowling shirts, but the wooden wall panelling feels
more bowling club than bowling alley. Heavy, dark, glass-
studded lampshades hang from antique-effect beams jutting
from the ceiling tiles. It's extremely atmospheric, as if David
Lynch, Mike Leigh and Krzysztof Kieslowski had built a place
to shoot movies in together.

The most striking waitress leans against the bar. Her hair is a bouffant puff of white candyfloss with a midnight-black fringe. Oversized specs magnify her eyes to massive pools that survey the room with mildly amused detachment. David, our waiter, brings us Polish appetizers: *pierogies* (filled dough parcels), a mound of sauerkraut, a jumbo sausage and dense potato dumplings. The star bite is the *kluski* pasta: thick egg noodles with poppy seeds and sour cream which have a texture that is as satisfying to bite as bubble-wrap is to pop. Minneapolis is a brewing city, and we all order pints of Grain Belt Premium.

I don't pay enough attention when I order my main course and choose a medium-sized rib. Medium size is 24oz. That's a pound and a half of cow hanging off a bone. It looks like the ribs that tip over Fred Flintstone's Stone Age buggy in the title sequence. The tastiest bit is the crunchy black stuff crusted around the bone. Wading through the spongy pink flesh begins to make me feel like I'm lost in a Dartmoor bog searching for an end, with a creeping sense of resignation as I realize that this is where I'll sink. I stuff a couple more forkfuls into my mouth, but it's too much. It doesn't feel like food any more. I give up. So do the singing granddads. Lu Sneider starts 'Making Whoopee'.

THE FORMOSA CAFÉ - *los angeles*

I gaze through the railway carriage window, past the banana leaves, to the stepped Deco parapet of the stark white studio lot opposite. Sixty years ago, Sam Goldwyn stood astride the parapet in the vicious mid-afternoon California sun and yelled at his writers to drop their cocktails and get back to work. I am in the Formosa Café on the corner of Formosa Avenue and Santa Monica Boulevard, Hollywood.

The lot facing us was the United Artists Studio, and the mob-run café gained a reputation there as the place where you could cash your pay cheque, order a cocktail and place a bet. Lana Turner supposedly dated the gangster proprietor.

Most of the black and crimson walls are hidden by signed photos of the stars who have haunted the place: Marilyn, Lucy and Desi, Groucho and Clifton Webb. Colonel Tom Parker chews a cigar butt, squinting from his grainy portrait. Above Elvis's favourite booth is a glass cabinet containing statuettes of him in various stages of obesity. He once tipped a waitress with a brand-new Cadillac. Our waitress grumbles that stars don't tip that way any more.

The food is eccentric. Essentially, it is Szechuan, but with weird combinations. The tuna tartar is on nachos. The stir-fried scallops are on sun-dried tomato linguini. It tastes as if there may be mayonnaise on the top. The flavours are all right, but we are sitting at the table where Sinatra scoffed chicken chow mein after scoring an Oscar for *From Here to Eternity*. We are not here for the food.

My friend who brought me here is a director but seems so

Brooklyn in this West Coast scene. In Hollywood tradition, conversation turns into gossip: who did what, who did whom and what did them in. The slightly vain lead singer, who was unhappy with his hair product when he saw the video edit and had his fauxhawk enhanced by computer; the beautiful and much sought-after dancer known as Supahead; groupie video libraries; how to shoot big butts; what PCP does to you; who's a good guy, who's a dick — everyone knows. There's the booth where that scene from *LA Confidential* was shot. I glance down at the Formica tabletop. Miles Davis soothes from the speakers. Hollywood isn't supposed to be real, but this place seems so vivid.

I know I will be back home in my empty flat in Glasgow in forty-eight hours. From this angle, it is that which does not seem real.

HEAVENLY HAMBURGERS- *palm springs*

I've been lying on my back, staring at the peeling ceiling of my flat for a couple of hours. There's been a leak. A numbing sense of lethargy overwhelms me when I come off tour. My languid veins miss the fizz of adrenalin they're served as I walk onstage each night. So I lie on the floorboards. Staring at the peeling ceiling.

I jump up from torpor. I split open my overloaded suitcase. Trousers stiff with desert dust and shirts damp with stage sweat leap out. Among the jumble is a crumpled paper cup, sticky with traces of root beer. Red palm trees circle the lip of the cup: silhouettes of the real ones in the In 'n' Out Burger parking lot on the freeway between Palm Springs and Los Angeles. I turn the cup over with my toe. There, under the base, is the secret message: John 3:16. Nothing indicates its presence or draws you to it. It's there for you to discover: 'For God so loved the world that he gave his only Son, that whoever believes in him should not perish but have eternal life.'

It's not exactly evangelical extremism, perhaps, but it is indicative of everyday Middle America: you don't have to look far to find a quote from the Bible. The reason could be on the bottom of the milkshake cups: Proverbs 3:5: 'Trust in the Lord with all thine heart; and lean not unto thine own understanding.' Maybe it's easier to let the Bible think for you. Or maybe God so loves the world that he wants to eat burgers and fries with us. It seems that way in the burger- and cheeseburger-wrapper small print: Revelation 3:20: 'Behold, I stand at the door, and knock: if any man hear my voice, and open the door, I will come in to him, and will sup with him, and he with me.'

If supping at In 'n' Out is OK by Him, it's OK by me. It is the best burger joint in California. Everything on the menu is very fresh and, since it pays its staff more than twice the minimum wage, there is none of the poisonous resentment among its workers that sees the staff at other fast-food joints spitting in your onion rings. At In 'n' Out there is a secret menu too. Ask for it 'animal style' and your burger comes fried in mustard with extra tasty gunk on the top.

California seems unreal and distant. I stick my finger in the sticky syrup. It's still sweet. I lie back down. I stare at the peeling ceiling for another few hours.

A blind man with wraparounds, pinched cheeks and a beanie hat hooks his stick over the crook of his arm and grips the granite wall on the corner of High Vennel and High Street, as if the icicle stings of rain will wash him into the iron murk of the Solway Firth. Wigtown is Scotland's 'book town'. The Box of Frogs sells kids' books. The Cauldron is culinary. The window of Tide Line is lined with titles such as *So You Want to Go Shooting?*, *The Gun Punt Adventure* and *The Complete Gundog*.

I'm hunting for a book about a Galloway character with nasty eating habits. In the sixteenth century, Sawney Bean and his incestuous clan feasted on the flesh of travellers they abducted on the west coast road to Glasgow. Limbs, like sickening hams, hung from the roof of their cave. I don't know how much is legend and how much is fact, but I have a vivid memory of a zealous guide on a primary school trip around Edinburgh Old Town describing their capture and execution in the Tolbooth — particularly the bit where, before absolute amputation, the men's 'privy members' were cut off and flung into the flames of the fires where the women were being burned alive.

I feel hungry. Every bookseller I chat to about Sawney recommends that I have a snack in the pink-painted Reading Lasses, the fantastically named women's studies bookshop and café. It is homely and welcoming. I am brought a thick plank of wood stacked with Galloway cheeses, chutneys and homemade bread dense with seeds. I open my book and flick through it, comforted by the reassuring flavours. A bowl of good soup can make you almost glad it is raining outside. The other customers are all reading, too.

They are mild and grey-haired, wearing warm, ramblers' fleeces. The dichotomy of good bookshops makes them a powerful environment: gentle, dusty places containing the extremes of human thought. I am reading about incestuous cannibals. I wonder what the ramblers are reading. It could be tragedy, violence, passion or needlecraft. Nothing in their expression gives it away. They quietly sip their coffee without raising their eyes from the page. Their faces are so ...

'What's the word that describes a face that is unreadable or gives nothing away?'

The woman with the inscrutable face next to me glances up from her page.

'Inscrutable.'

Feathery fuzz blows from fresh-leaved trees behind me in Soho Square. I walk along Frith Street past William Hazlitt's house and the tattoo parlour. The street is sticky from the night before. The puddles are opaque and milky. Ronnie Scott's is having a facelift at 47. The cast of *Mary Poppins* flows through the stage door of the Prince Edward Theatre. Café tables rest rickety on the grubby pavement outside Little Italy, Bar Italia and Nino's. A woman in Chanel sunglasses and a fleece cups her hand around her cappuccino for warmth. A traffic warden is giving a fire engine a parking ticket.

I turn on to Old Compton Street, dodging the men in aprons and scowls pushing overloaded hand-trolleys. To the left, on Greek Street, grey net curtains blow limply in the spring breeze behind the unlit lightboxes. To the right is Café Bertaux.

I'm greeted by a woman with a polka-dot scarf, a brunette bouffant swirl like a Danish pastry and a welcoming voice like *café au lait*. She tells me she will bring my coffee and tart upstairs to me. Generations of feet have worn the lino from the steps. The air is saturated with the louche charisma of Quentin Crisp's Soho. The Formica table tops each have a couple of tulips in a half-pint tumbler. A Greaser couple sip tea. She has a box jacket striped like a Mint Imperial and Betty Page bangs. He has a quiff, Malcolm X specs and clumsy gold on every finger. A group of stripy shirts chatter over a mound of spent crockery. They are compiling a Rich List. 'I'm looking for colour and humour.' 'I'm looking after my expense account.'

A Virginia Woolf in a floral frock sits by a man with a Panama

hat. On my right, a young designer leafs through her portfolio and sticks a spoon in the pastry decadence of her strawberry tart. Mine is a quivering tower of luscious fruit and *crème anglaise*. The rich flavours aren't obscured by sweetness. Raspberries squirt acid clarity across the custard. This is not something to guzzle, but sensation to be savoured in nibbles so no flavour escapes the opportunity to be tasted.

Bertaux is the antithesis of chain coffee-shops. The shabby quirkiness and character cannot be franchised and replicated on every high street. It's also expensive. It's a place to take someone you like. Someone who appreciates a treat.

Cologne sets itself aside by the way they serve beer there. In the rest of Germany, it froths over the lips of heavy, dimpled stein, like thick glass buckets with a handle on the side. Kölsch is served in a slender tumbler called a Kölsch-*Stange* that looks more like a test tube. I'm drinking with Parker, our sound engineer, on a bench outside the Pfaffen Bräuerei on the corner of the cobbled Heumarkt. It's drizzling, and full inside, so we look for somewhere else to eat.

The Bräuhaus Sunner im Walfisch is also full. The headwaiter twirls the handles of his moustache, waving four plates of sausages and potato. 'They came from Denmark. I am sorry.' He squeezes us into a heaving bench below a wrought-iron two-headed Byzantine eagle clutching a light bulb in each claw. We order a Kölsch Tower, three litres tall, like a beaker from a chemistry lab, with a tap at the bottom. The three people sitting on our left like that we like Kölsch. 'You like Kölsch?' Yes. This is very funny. They laugh with big Santa Klaus ho-ho-ho's. We order Kölsch Kaviar. It's a cold black pudding, rusty red with square flecks of white fat, mildly spicy and delicious on slices of onion and rye. The jolly Germans notice we're eating. 'You like German food?' Yes. This is also very funny. Ho ho ho.

My Rhineland roast is intense: slices of beef with thick, sticky raisin *jus* and potato dumplings that have the texture of large gnocchi. Parker has a pork knuckle – a large primal bone of oven-twisted meat and crackling glued to the plate with potato mash that is more butter than potato. Eating it is a physical activity. He carves with the serrated blade and slips. A ball of gristle ricochets from his plate, bounces off the table on to the floor. The Jolly Munchers explode. Guffaws of food bits and happy spittle rain through the air. 'Fast Eddie!' Ho ho ho. 'Fast Eddie!' We join in the laughter briefly. We don't get it. 'Fast Eddie!' Yeah. Ho ho ho.

We pour another Kölsch and finish our food. They're still laughing, beaming at us as if we're going to be funny again. We're not. We talk about Parker's new digital mixing desk. Their mood sinks. They put their glum coats on. One turns back hopefully.

'Fast Eddie?'

Parker forces a smile.

'Fast Eddie.'

SLIPPING DOWN THE SCOVILLE SCALE - *lisbon*

I climb the steep Calçada da Glória by the side of the funicular railway tracks, my leather soles slipping off marble cobbles that are like uneven cubes of volcanic ice. One foot goes, and I grab the broken rail. This dramatic urban gorge slices through the old town of Lisbon. Graffiti covers the walls in spaghetti swirling scrawls of spray-can anarchist colour. I meet Parker outside Alfaia on the corner of Rue do Diario de Notaçias and Travessa da Queimada. The aluminium chair is on such a gradient that, as I sit, I slide into its back.

A selection of cheese, ham and olives is brought to the table. It is worth going to Lisbon just to eat Azeitao cheese. The ancient, muslin-wrapped rind looks like the skin of an Egyptian mummy. The top has been sliced off and a tiny spoon stands in the runny interior. It is made in Portugal's highest mountains from raw, unpasteurized ewe's milk, using Cardoon thistle instead of rennet. We dribble it like honey over the fresh bread, the sweet pungency dilating our nostrils as it coats the roof of our mouths. A purple plate of octopus appears, peppered with a mild chilli. Parker tells me about the Scoville scale, which is used to grade the heat of chillies. A jalapeno is around 3,000, a bell pepper is zero. What we're eating would just make a couple of hundred.

On our right is the window of the kitchen. Rows of silvery bass stare past us at the sun-faded photographs of last year's hair-dos in the hairdresser's window over the street. The chef sees us and sticks thumb and forefinger into the eyes of a pointy-snouted sea salmon, holding it up for us to see, gaping the gills in a floppy grin.

We order fish. The Caldeirada de Peixes do Mar is described as 'different slices of sea fish sliced into pieces to be cooked in tomato, onion, garlic, white wine, peppers, altogether with potatoes'. Crude chunks of unknown fish swim in a sauce that tastes like it has simmered overnight. In case the deep-yellow potatoes haven't absorbed every flavour, there are soppy slices of bread at the bottom, under the bones. We scrape the last dribble of Azeitao from the rind. We drip the last drop of red wine. The cobbles seem slippier on the way down.

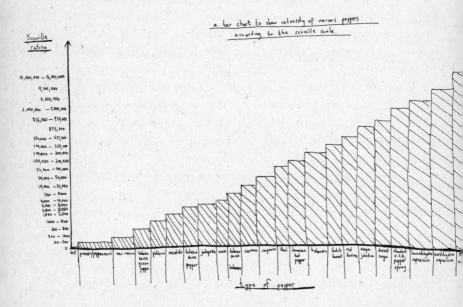

a bar chart to show intensity of various peppers according to the scoville scale.

BEMUSED TO DEATH - *beverly hills*

At Mr Chow, Beverly Hills, they don't like to give you a menu. 'I could go down to the vault, see what I find,' sniffs the waiter. He has the preppy perfectionism of a young Patrick Bateman. We let him choose what we'll eat. The foul-mouthed heir to a billion dollars of oil money sits at the table on our right. It's the birthday of a woman at the table on our left. It's hard to guess which birthday. It could be anything between forty and eighty, as her face is a rigid surgical mask: any expression not sliced away by the scalpel has been frozen with botox. There are no chopsticks on the table, but chilled droplets condense on the shiny surface of a huge silver basin of Veuve Cliquot by a massive ball of lilies. A latenight-chat-show host sits opposite. My friend tells me that on a celebrity scale of one to ten, this is a Monday night two, as there isn't a Clooney, Cruise or Spielberg.

The waiter tells us he's bringing a Special Surprise. In the meantime, it's Showtime. An older Chinese chef wheels a linen-clad trolley into the centre of the room and raises a huge mound of dough above his head. He stretches it, then slaps it off the table in a violent cloud of flour, demanding the gaze of every eye in the place. He stretches it into a long sausage, doubles it and twirls it around like a lasso Yo-Yo. He repeats this until he has a tangle of noodles held in the air to an explosion of applause. A couple of minutes later, we're eating them. They're Mr Chow's Special Noodles with a meat sauce that tastes like bolognaise laced with soya sauce. Then comes the Special Surprise. It's frog's legs. They're battered and fried with chilli. They must have been muscular frogs, as there's lots of flesh on the greenish bones. What do frogs taste of? Well, these ones taste of chilli. The best thing we are brought is the duck, which is wonderful: as soft and rich as molten chocolate. Everything tastes so good you can't tell what it is. There's a wee bit of snobby arrogance amongst the waiters. They tell you what you'll eat, then don't give a toss whether you enjoy it or not. My friend is bemused by the glamour: 'People come here for status. The food's good, but this place tastes like death to me.'

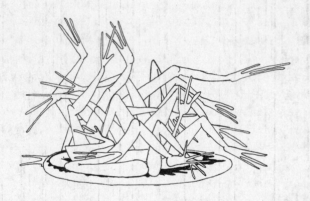

Mr Chow is the contemporary equivalent of the Formosa Café – a star hang-out that serves westernized Chinese food. This was the first time I tried frog. I like to try everything. Some things that are alien to my palate aren't as weird as I expect them to be. Frog was familiar, not particularly shocking or surprising, but then it was crusted in jalapenos. On the streets of Bangkok, there is a lot of fast food. Carts with hot plates and grills fry and toss in amongst the tooting tuk-tuk scooter taxis and hawkers advertising bars with ping-pong-ball floor-shows. The tastiest treat is the stinkiest. Durian is known as the king of fruit, is huge, spiky and smells like an overloaded bin bag on a summer's day. The custard-coloured, pulpy, stringy flesh isn't sweet but is rich and tastes like no other fruit. It is banned from a lot of buildings because of its stench.

The most alien snacks to a Western palate are the deep-fried insects. We had just met a baby elephant when we spotted them. A handcart with a deep-fat fryer had stacks of them under grass. There were different types – some large, some small. They were sold in paper bags like an old-fashioned quarter of sweets. There were beetles, grasshoppers and a few I didn't recognize. We tried a poke of what I think were locusts. They were fried a deep brown and didn't taste too bizarre – just deep-fried and crunchy. Once you stopped thinking so hard about what was in your mouth, it was like eating a bag of crisps except that, every now and then, a brittle serrated leg would get stuck between your teeth.

I love nature. My legs and arse ache from the saddle, but I am elated. This is the first time I've ridden a horse, yet cantering across the canyon in Malibu felt like I'd ridden them for thousands of years. Pelicans fly low over the Pacific Ocean. Three dolphins leap through the surface, twisting in the air like kids playing on a trampoline. The outcrop where I stand is covered in wild mussels, wet-black like patent-leather bubbles on the salt-carved rock. A wave thuds suddenly to an end and foam swirls around my knees. The wooden sign tells me that it is an offence to eat these mussels or sell them to anyone else who may want to eat them. They're probably poisonous, loaded with sewage juice or heavy metals, but they look so gorgeous clinging to the rocks, wet and slightly parted, as if inviting me gently to nibble the button of flesh peeping out. Haze, it's all a beautiful haze; I'm a delirious kid from Glasgow who can't believe where he is.

We get into the car and drive back a couple of miles to the Paradise Cove Beach Café. Fading photos tell stories of handsome lifeguards racing into pre-war surf and beautiful girls in heavy woollen bathers lined along the sand like a Busby Berkeley chorus line. We sit outside at a plastic table. The bus boy brings us a portion of mussels and fries that is obscene in size — a bucket of each. A flock of forty gulls lands on the furniture around us. Their amber eyes consider us. They consider the fries. They consider us to be no danger, and a big guy flaps on to the table, vicious and ungainly. The beak is like a yellow, hooked fisherman's knife with a broken hole behind a blood-red splat. Eight fries in one snap. This is one big bird who does not give a damn. This guy is scared of nothing: certainly not me. I clap my hands, and he cocks his head as if saying, 'Oh, purleeease...' before snapping another beakful. I throw a cardboard carton of milk towards him. He catches it in his beak and swallows it. His pals watch him, waiting for their turn. This is like Bodega Bay, but a little more sinister. We grab our mussels and fries and fly inside to the safety of the manmade world. I hate nature.

BEWARE THE WHITE WIDOW -*utrecht*

Workmen are re-cobbling Mariastraat, sweeping grit between the stones. They wear roller-blader's kneepads and thick wooden clogs, the toe-points scuffed flat and rough. The faint tick of our back wheels follows us across Utrecht to the canal. It is a small university city, like a pretty miniature Amsterdam without the red-light tourism. The counter-culture is high-street: a few innocuous coffeeshops politely selling pre-rolled joints, their heavy-headed customers sedately watching the World Cup. A goal. A silent goal. Beware the White Widow.

We lock our bikes with a hundred others above the Oudegracht – the old canal that runs north to south through the city, which is lined with cafés and restaurants – and walk down the wooden steps to De Oude Muntkelder: The Old Coin Cellar Pancake House.

We sit on the edge of the brown-green water, sunlight dappling gently through the soft-leaved trees, dancing in the wake of a putting barge. Fallen pollen films the surface like stubble in a sink of lukewarm water, scattered by a splashing family of mallards. Graceful dreads of matted weed drift by. Bob says he wants to live here. 'I could get a flat by the water. Paddle to the pub.'

The waitress presents each of us with a twelve-inch gold disc. The pillowy-soft batter tapers to a crisp, crunchy edge.

I could not decide whether I wanted bacon and apple or bacon and cheese. Each sounded good, so I ordered all three fillings. It is a crowded pancake. The streaks of bacon and slivers of apple are contrasting characters, but couple well. His salty directness is offset by her sweet, forgiving nature, making their relationship complex and complementary. Bacon gets on well with cheese too. They're so similar – vigorous and rude, wrapped together in sweaty excitement. But cheese and apple are vile to each other. Bacon brings out their sickly bitching contradictions, their flavours fighting for his attention, spoiling each other, and awkward in the pancake like a mistress and wife sharing a train carriage with their boorish lover. I love the drama. I tear off a piece and toss it to a drake. He beats the water and snaps his bill. He loves it too.

What am I thinking? Apple as bacon's wife? Cheese as a mistress? It's just food. Beware the White Widow.

The Bura wind blows from the peaks of the Dalmatian Alps to the Adriatic, dry, cold and inescapable. It hisses through every crack and crevice, through winter and summer clothes and the gaps in the wooden walls of the smokehouses where Croatian *prsut* ham is cured. It is what gives the ham its distinct character. Although it is a cousin of *serrano* and *prosciutto*, it is unique, this lean and salty dry meat, not as exhausting on the tongue as its Italian and Spanish relatives. It is wrapped around a scallop on a swirl of polenta infused with Istrian black truffle, a potent and refined set of flavours. We have gone out for dinner in Zagreb with the guys who run Dancing Bear, our Croatian record label. 'The staff are a little nervous. They think you're opera stars,' says Silvije. 'It's the name, Franz Ferdinand.'

There is a noticeable Austro-Hungarian flavour to the beautiful city, a careless grace and grandeur like a supermodel nipping out to Lidl in her trackie bottoms and vest after a heavy night. I try to thank the waiter for the delicious, home-made, beetroot-stuffed ravioli made from poppy-seed flour. '*Hvala.*' It comes out more like 'Hoovallurgh'. Everyone laughs. My accent is bad. I try again. No. It does not come naturally.

We are in the vaulted brick basement of the Sorriso restaurant, where the speakers seep music that sounds like eighties power ballads sung with more consonants. It is a guy called Massimo, who is massive here. Imagine the long, reverberating snares and saccharine synths of Foreigner's 'I Want To to Know What Love Is' or Berlin's 'Take My Breath Away' behind the earnest crooning of what sounds like 'szjckvcmpscljmj europsoj bajbji'. The Croats all suck on domestic Ronhill fags between courses. The wine is Istrian too and very good, but not as interesting as the *biska* liqueur, a mistletoe brandy served in a thistle-shaped glass, which perfectly concludes a great meal.

We wander through the main square, which is still busy with trams. Zoran points out the defiant equestrian statue of Josip Jelačić, leader of the Croatian resistance in the nineteenth century. 'His sword always points towards our enemies. He used to face north towards Hungary. We moved him to face south towards Serbia in 1990.'

'Where will they point him next?' I ask.

'I don't know' laughs Zoran. 'Probably Slovenia.'

The twin-propeller plane looked as if it was made of Lego. It flew us from Gdansk to Edinburgh this morning, our equipment strapped to the floor with rope webbing between us and the pilot. In-flight catering was watery, cold, scrambled eggs and cold bacon. The fat had congealed into hard white tears on the edge of the plastic tray. So, I'm hungry as we drive up the muddy track that leads to the artists' enclosure at T in the Park under evil, July winter clouds. Our tour bus, 15 tonnes of tinted excess, passes the security checkpoint where I stood on a parched summer's day three years ago, holding my guitar in its protective bin bag, as the security guard, after checking his list of bands, said, 'Sorry son, I don't think you're playing - you shouldn't be in this area.'

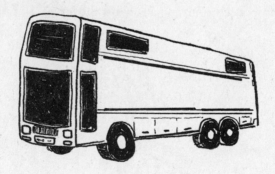

We don't have time to eat. We go straight to a press conference. It feels like February, but I keep my sunglasses on. It's not that I think it's cool. It's not. There are just too many eyes to make any meaningful contact with. A thousand flashes, a hundred questions. 'How does it feel to be back at T?' I'm so hungry. We walk back through the rain to the catering tent. The caterers are Popcorn, who are always good. I glance at the blackboard, registering braised lamb shanks and five-spice duck with ginger greens, as I rush to the queue. I stand behind Edith Bowman and in front of Sophie Ellis-Bextor, who is holding a cute fiery-haired toddler in her arms.

I take some tuna to a table covered in a tartan tablecloth. I bite and there is a faint itchy tingle on the roof of my mouth. I had the same tingle two days ago when I ate a chicken salad in Serbia that had peanut butter in the dressing. I'm allergic and threw up for hours that night. I spit it out. It's probably nothing, but I can't risk it. The gig has to be good. I glance at the cakes instead. Amazing. A dark, gooey pecan pie, sugar-dusted lemon tart and a dense chocolate thing. Oh, yes! Let me eat cake! I'm a rock star! If I want to eat nothing but cake I can! I pile the bowl high, guiltily glancing around, looking for Security, still expecting to hear, 'Sorry son - you shouldn't be in this area.'

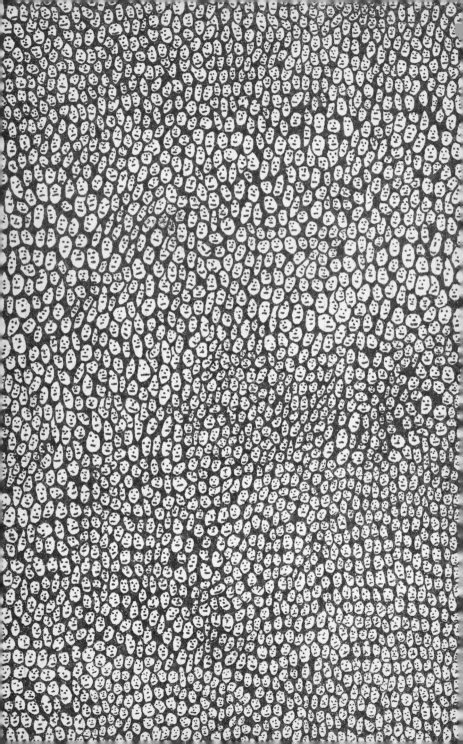

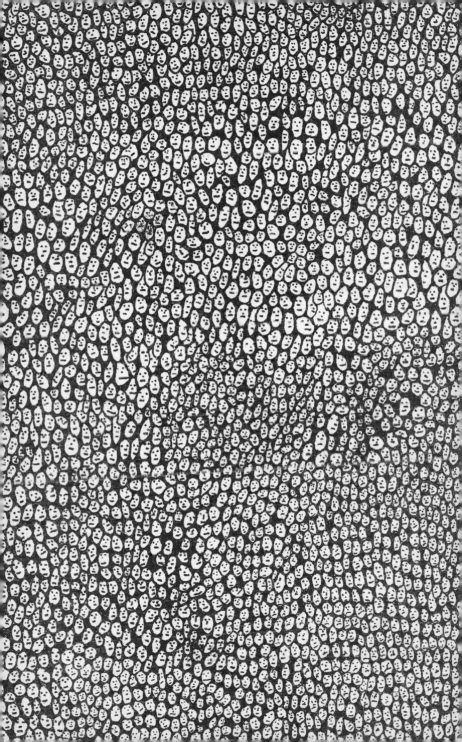

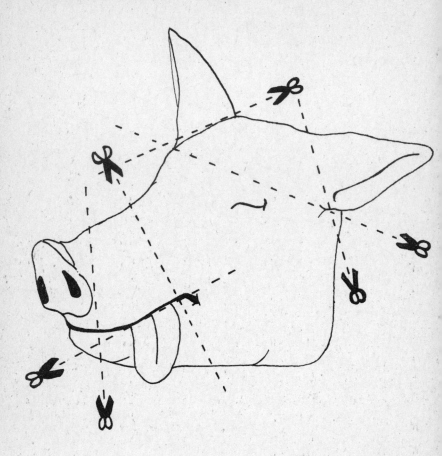

I want to introduce you to this fellow. He's the special guest at weddings and film premières. We put money in his mouth because it's lucky. You usually find him in traditional Korean markets like this one. Ah, here we are: this guy isn't together, which is a shame. It's better when he's whole. The tiny old lady behind the stall pulls the plastic carrier bag from the top of the pot, revealing a jumble of chopped snout, ears and brain. It's a pig's head, a little grey and boiled. You can try if you want. No, I think I'll save myself for the Kimchi pancakes. Thanks.

We're wandering around the market in Incheon, Korea. Jean tells me that it's quiet today. The stallholders are normally quite animated, shouting and singing at you about how good their food is. 'We Koreans are more like Italians, very different from the Japanese. Their culture is based around hiding your emotions. We like to express ourselves and do it loudly.'

We pass a stall with trestle tables overloaded with dried fish. Big ones speared below the gills in a row, staring from sunken eyes like a dozen marine mummies. Tiny silver ones like metal-shop filings in a sack. Christine points at a half-barrel of microscopic shrimps. We eat some with Kimchi. They are soaked for a very long time in salt and all of the juice comes out, and the flavour is magnificent. I bring my face close to a bucket of clams in seawater. Semi-opaque tubes protrude from the shells; softly swaying as if they're mildly curious about this new environment they've found themselves in. One gently breaks the surface like a periscope and shoots an arc of water past my left ear.

The next stall sells sweets and birthday cakes made from sticky rice, decorated with turrets and vivid colours. I try a bit of the rice sweet, which is mild and sticky, near sushi rice in consistency, but dark brown. A woman feeds a pot-bellied stove with flat bread that puffs up into hollow balls with the heat. Medicinal stalls sell pickled ginseng root suspended in jars of sinister fluid, like limbs preserved in formaldehyde.

Sweet pumpkin soup simmers in cauldrons next to bubbling sweet bean paste.

Then we notice the Russian bar. The sign is in Cyrillic and every inch of wall space is covered in graffiti. This is the hangout of Russian and Filipino sailors. Incheon is a busy port. Most of the graffiti is also in Cyrillic, but a few words in English jump from the scrawl, notably 'I will not forgive' and 'violent'. There's a guitar propped up in the corner, also covered in graffiti.

We sit down for Kimchi dumplings and pancakes. The spicy fermented cabbage gives you a sensational rush. Sweat covers your skin instantly. In the dense humid air, it's refreshing, like having a cool damp cloth laid over your entire body. The TV is playing a wobbly video of a Russian station. Cut to a trailer for a stunt show. A man clutches a wound on his forehead. Cut to a Lada driving off the edge of a bridge. Cut to a man in an orange boiler suit and crash helmet shouting at something coming towards him. Cut to another Lada running over the man in the orange boiler suit. Cut to a man shooting the lock off a shed. Cut to his heavy features. Cut to them being punched. There's no Hollywood shine to disguise the grim brutality.

A sailor with a blond crew cut stares ahead of him. Jean smokes a long, anaemic government-issue fag. I bite again, evaporating quietly by the guitar.

END OF THE ROAD - *prague*

'Hey, Blondie! You want to go to titty bar?'

'No, you're all right, pal.'

'Hey, Blondie, it's good titty bar!'

'I'm sure it is.'

'What's wrong, Blondie? You not like titties?'

'Look, pal, tits are great, but titty bars are crap, so will you just fuck off?'

This is Prague. It's time to stop writing about food. There's a booth selling sweet dough that has been wrapped around a metal cylinder, roasted, then coated with sugar, steam rising from the hollow stack like smoke from an Ottoman chimney. I'm in the main square by the astrological clock. It seems to be on the side of a church, in a marriage of superstition and religion. The queue for the sweet chimneys is about fifteen long when the stallholder announces that he is shutting. He has run out of dough.

Disappointment ripples along the queue like a domino rally. It reaches two teenage British girls with pink faces and heavy backpacks. It's too much for them. Consternation propels them to the lip of the stall, where the last of the chimneys are being handed over. They have an unquestionable sense of privately educated self-assurance. Girl One fixes the stallholder with an upturned nose and schoolteacher gaze. She barks like a vicar's wife.

'You can't possibly close! We're leaving tomorrow!'

The stallholder glances at her.

'I said we're leaving TOMORROW.'

Girl Two pulls an anxious face that begs 'please' like a dog at a dinner table.

'Sorry, we have no more,' says the stallholder.

'God, I just can't believe these people,' huffs Girl One as they turn their backs on the chimneys.

I think something similar. I don't know how many times Prague has been invaded, but tonight it seems to have been invaded by wankers: British wankers, German wankers, North African wankers and American wankers.

A tourist in his early twenties is explaining to another tourist in her early twenties that he is not a tourist: he is a 'traveller'. They have a tourist map spread on the café table in front of them by the English translation of the menu. He is saying that his experience is richer. He looks, smells and acts like a tourist. I don't get it. Because he stays in a hostel rather than a hotel is the veritas more veritable? Or is he just a git? I'm a tourist. I tour the world. I don't feel I have to excuse myself. The travelling bit is dull. In my mind, it's standing around baggage belts hoping that my case hasn't been lost again. Of course I'm a bloody tourist. I don't have the insider's perspective. I feel like a stranger everywhere I go. I like that perspective. In restaurants, I love to sit with my back to the wall so I can watch the other diners. You see what authors and filmmakers attempt to capture but in real time. Just because you're a tourist, it doesn't mean you have to behave obnoxiously. If anything, you should behave better than you normally would. Two Great British clichés are 1) to presume that if you are in someone else's country, you can do what the hell you like and 2) that if you are in a band, it's obligatory to behave like a boorish thug.

The festival site feels like an abandoned Cosmonaut holiday camp. Loose tiles fall into the paddling pool. The rusted umpire's chair has toppled over by the overgrown tennis courts. In the murk of the surrounding forest are shadows of buildings that could have been dormitories or centrifugal test chambers. Tinny loudspeakers broadcast bloc versions of easy classics: the Cornetto tune, 'Edelweiss', the one about the meatball rolling down a hill, all with soft Czech vocals. There's a huge home-welded spit and brazier. The fire has settled to steady embers and two men grunt as they lift a meat-covered pole onto a ratchet system connected to an old engine. The meat must weigh more than either of them. It looks incredible, like a medieval feast transported to the mid-twentieth century. Ministry are setting up on stage one. A tech is erecting the skull-encrusted microphone stand. The Pet Shop Boys are setting up on stage two. They are working out how the dancers can burst from the neon-lit white cube. We're somewhere in the middle.

In two weeks we'll play the Reading and Leeds festivals: the climax of a year and a half of touring. It has been an intense adventure, crawling across the planet, performing to millions of people. Each night as I walk on to the dark stage, the white light of the strobes and the white noise of the crowd send a wave of adrenalin to my heart, setting off a vascular explosion that feels like it could kill me. The blood feels like it'll burst from the fingertips as the arteries fling it through my flesh. Before my pick flicks the strings, my toes have already flipped me into the air, hovering over the boards in the fast-frame of anticipation. It's time to stop. You can only play the same songs a certain number of times before you get bored. It's time to stop, because it is still exciting. It's time to stop, because I need to live somewhere that isn't a bus or a hotel room. It's time to stop touring, so it's time to stop writing about food.

What I eat at home isn't interesting. It's the same as anyone else.

Some useful addresses from this book, in order of appearance:

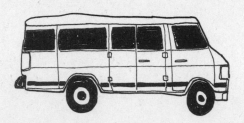

Avra Estatorio, the Greek fish grill referred to in 'Purple Goram', 141 East 48th Street, New York, NY 10017, tel. +1 212 759 8550, www.avrany.com. Open for lunch Fri from noon; brunch Sat & Sun 11 a. m.–4 p.m.; dinner Mon–Sat 5 p.m.–12 a.m., Sun 5 p.m.–11 p.m.

Las Manitas Avenue Café, Tex-Mex diner, 211 Congress Avenue, Austin, TX 78701, tel. +1 512 472 9357. Open 7 a.m.– 4 p.m. weekdays, 7 a.m.–2.30 p.m. weekends

Freshness Burger have various stores throughout Tokyo and Japan. Their website is www.freshnessburger.co.jp

In 'n' Out Burger have fifty stores in Los Angeles. Their website is www.In-n-Out.com

The Ocean Aire, seafood restaurant with a steakhouse style, 1700 7th Avenue, Seattle, Washington, WA 98101, tel. +1 206 267 2277, fax +1 206 267 2156. Open Mon–Thurs 11.30 a.m– 10 p.m., Fri 11.30 a.m.–11 p.m., Sat & Sun 5 p.m.–10 p.m.

Country Station Sushi Café, 2140 Mission & Sycamore, San Francisco, CA, tel. +1 415 861 0972, fax +1 415 864 3119. Open Mon–Thurs 4.30 p.m.–9.30 p.m., Fri & Sat 4.30 p.m.–9 p.m.

Keen's Chop House or Steak House (they have changed their name to the latter since my visit), 72 West 36th Street, New York, NY 10018, tel. +1 212 947 2626, www.keensteakhouse.com. Open Mon–Fri 11.45 a.m.–10.30 p.m., Sat 5 p.m.–10.30 p.m., Sun 5 p.m.–9 p.m.

Blue Ribbon Brasserie, American food, 97b Sullivan Street, New York, tel. +1 212 274 0404. Open 4 p.m.–4 a.m. daily

Chez Jean, traditional French restaurant, 8 Rue St-Lazare, 9th arrondissement, Paris, tel. +33 1 48786273. Open 8 p.m. 10.30 p.m. weekdays, 12 p.m.–2 p.m. weekends

Le Taroudant II, Moroccan restaurant, 8 Rue Aristide Bruant, 18th arrondissement, Paris, tel. +33 1 42649581. Open daily 11.30 a.m.–2.30 p.m., 7 p.m.–11 p.m.

Clignancourt food market, Avenue de la Porte de Clignancourt, 18th arrondissement, Paris

Rasa, Indian restaurant, 56 Stoke Newington Church Street, London N16 0AR, tel. 0207 249 0344. Open Mon–Thurs 6 p.m.–10.30 p.m., Fri–Sat 6 p.m.–11.30 p.m.

Mother India's Café, 28 Westminster Terrace, Glasgow G3 7RU, tel. 0141 221 1663, fax 0141 221 2217; or 1355 Argyle Street, West End, Glasgow G3 8AD, tel. 0141 339 9145. Open Mon–Sun 12 p.m.–2 p.m., 5.30 p.m.–11 p.m.

The Buttery, Scottish/French restaurant, 652 Argyle Street, West End, Glasgow G3 8UF, tel. 0141 221 8188, fax 0141 204 4639, ia.fleming@btopenworld.com. Open Tues–Fri 12 p.m.–10 p.m., Sat 6 p.m.–10 p.m.

Dickson's Pork Shop, 162 Dean Road, South Shields, NE33 4AQ, tel. 0191 456 4290. Open Mon, Tues, Thurs and Fri 8.30 a.m.–3.15 p.m., Wed and Sat 8.30 a.m.– 2 p.m.

Munich Christmas Market, Marienplatz, Munich. Open Mon–Fri 10 a.m.–8.30 p.m., Sat 9 a.m.–8.30 p.m., Sun 10 a.m.–7.30 p.m.

Antica Trattoria della Pesa, traditional Milanese cuisine, Viale Pasuvio 10, Milan 20154, tel. +39 265 55741, fax +39 265 55413. Open Mon–Sat 12.30 p.m.–2.30 p.m., 7.30 p.m.–11 p.m., closed Sun

Casa Alcalde, Calle Mayor 19, 20003 Donostia, San Sebastián, tel. +34 943 426216

La Broche, experimental Spanish cuisine, Calle de Miguel Angel 29–31, Madrid 28010, tel. +34 913 993437, fax +34 913 993778, www.labroche.com. Open Mon–Fri 2 p.m.–4 p.m., 9 p.m.–11.30 p.m., closed Sat, Sun and throughout August

Sean's Panaroma, Australian restaurant, 270 Campbell Parade, Bondi Beach, Sydney, New South Wales, NSW 2026, tel. +61 2 9365 4924, fax +61 2 9130 7843, panaroma @ozemail.com.au, www.seanspanaroma.com.au. Open for lunch Sat & Sun 12 p.m.–3 p.m.; dinner Wed–Sat from 6:30 p.m.

Harry's Singapore Chilli Crab Restaurant, Triple Ace Bar, Level 1, 198 Elizabeth Street, Sydney, New South Wales, NSW 2000, tel. +61 2 9281 5565, www.harryschillicrab.com.au

Bigmouth, Australian restaurant, 168 Acland Street, St Kilda, Melbourne, Victoria, VIC 3182, tel. +61 3 9534 4611. Open 8 a.m.–11.30 p.m. daily

Temple Street Night Market, Yau Ma Tei, Kowloon, Hong Kong. Open from 2 p.m. daily

Nasi Lemak, Adam Road Food Center, located between the Junction of Dunearn Road and Adam Road, Singapore

Porção, Brazilian grill and barbecue, Avenue Infante Dom Henrique, s/numero, Atero do Flamengo, Rio de Janeiro, tel. +55 21 3461 9020, www.porcao.com.br. Open Mon–Thurs 11.30 a.m.–midnight, Fri, Sat and holidays 11.30 a.m.–1 a.m.

St Elmo Market, St Elmo Avenue, Buenos Aires

Bar Dorrego, Calle Defensa 1098, Buenos Aires, tel. +54 11 4361 0141

La Brigada, Argentinian parilla grill, Estado Unidos 465, Bolivar, San Telmo, Buenos Aires, tel. +5411 4351 5557. Open 12 p.m.– 3 p.m., 8 p.m.–midnight daily

Peter Pan Donut and Pastry Shop, 727 Manhattan Avenue, Brooklyn, NY 11222, USA, tel +1 718 389-3676

Dumont, 432 Union Avenue, Williamsburg, Brooklyn, NY 11206, tel. +1 718 486 7717, www.dumontrestaurant.com. Open for dinner Mon–Sun 6 p.m.–11 p.m., lunch Mon–Fri 11 a.m.– 3 p.m., brunch Sat & Sun 11 a.m.–3.30 p.m.

Les Halles, 411 Park Avenue South (between 28th & 29th Streets), New York, NY 10016, tel. +1 212 679 4111, fax. +1 212 779 0679, www.leshalles.net. Open Mon–Sat 8 a.m.–midnight, Sun 11 a.m.–midnight

Old Ebbitt Grill, 675 15th Street, N. W., Washington, DC 20005, tel. +1 202 347 4800, www.ebbitt.com. Open Mon–Fri 7.30 a.m.–1 a.m., Sat & Sun 8.30 a.m.–1 a.m.

Schwartz's Charcuterie Hébraïque de Montréal, 3895 Saint-Laurent Boulevard, Montreal, Quebec H2W 1X9, tel. +1 514 842 4813, fax. +1 514 842 0800. Open Mon–Thurs & Sun 8 a.m.– 12.30 a.m., Fri 8 a.m.–1.30 a.m., Sat 8 a.m.–2.30 a.m.

The Done Right Inn 861 Queen Street, West, Toronto, Ontario M6J 1G4, tel.+1 416 703 0405

Banu, Iranian restaurant, 777 Queen Street, West, Toronto, Ontario M6J 1G1, tel.+1 416 777 2268

Nye's Polonaise Room, 112 East Hennepin Ave, Minneapolis, tel. +1 612 379 2021. Open Mon–Sat 11 a.m.–2 a.m., Sun 4 p.m.–2 a.m.

Formosa Café, 7156 Santa Monica Blvd, West Hollywood, CA 90046, tel. +1 323 850 9050. Open Mon–Fri 4 p.m.–2 a.m., Sat & Sun 6 p.m.–2 a.m.

Maison Bertaux, a special French café known for its excellent coffee and pain au chocolat, 28 Greek Street, Soho, London, W1D 5DD, tel. 0207 437 6007. Open Mon–Sat 8.30 a.m.–11 p.m., Sun 9 a.m.–9 p.m.

Reading Lasses, Bookshop/Café, 17 South Main Street, Wigtown, Wigtownshire, DG8 9EH, tel. 01988 403266, fax. 01988 403266,www.reading-lasses.com. Open Mon–Sat 10 a.m.–5 p.m., closed Sundays

Bräuhaus Sunner im Walfisch, Saltzgasse 13, 50667 Cologne, tel. +49 221 2577879, fax +49 221 2577809. Open Mon–Thurs 5 p.m.–1. a.m., Fri 3 p.m.–2 a.m., Sat & Sun 11 a.m.–2 a.m.

Alfaia Restaurante, Travessa da Queimada, 22, 1200–365 Lisbon, tel. + 351 213 461 232. Open Mon–Sat 12 p.m.–2 a.m., Sun 6.30 p.m.–2 a.m.

Mr Chow, 344 North Camden Drive, Beverly Hills, CA 90210, tel. +1 310 278 9911, fax +1 310 278 4671, www.mrchow.com

Paradise Cove Beach Café, 28128 Pacific Coast Highway, Malibu, CA 90265, tel. +1 310 457 2503, www.paradisecovemalibu.com/beachcafe

De Oude Muntkelder, Oude Gracht a/d Wef 112, 3511 AW Utrecht, tel. 030 2 31 67 73, www.deoudemuntkelder.nl. Open Mon–Sun 12 p.m.–9 p.m.

Sorriso, Zagreb, Boskovićeva 11, Croatia, tel. +385 1 487 63 92, fax: +385 1 487 63 93, www.sorriso.hr. Open Mon–Sat 10 a.m.–12 a.m., closed Sun

Above information correct at time of going to press. Any omissions, or subsequent alterations, in the above listings will be made good in future impressions.

Acknowledgements

Helen Pidd at the *Guardian* had the idea of the column and its name, and is a patient, supportive and wonderful editor. Thanks to Andy Knowles, who I hoped might scribble down a few sketches but instead spent hours creating oblique and beautiful illustrations. Thanks to Juliet Annan and John Hamilton at Penguin for their encouragement and patience.

FOR THE BEST IN PAPERBACKS, LOOK FOR THE

In every corner of the world, on every subject under the sun, Penguin represents quality and variety—the very best in publishing today.

For complete information about books available from Penguin—including Penguin Classics, Penguin Compass, and Puffins—and how to order them, write to us at the appropriate address below. Please note that for copyright reasons the selection of books varies from country to country.

In the United States: Please write to *Penguin Group (USA), P.O. Box 12289 Dept. B, Newark, New Jersey 07101-5289* or call 1-800-788-6262.

In the United Kingdom: Please write to *Dept. EP, Penguin Books Ltd, Bath Road, Harmondsworth, West Drayton, Middlesex UB7 0DA.*

In Canada: Please write to *Penguin Books Canada Ltd, 90 Eglinton Avenue East, Suite 700, Toronto, Ontario M4P 2Y3.*

In Australia: Please write to *Penguin Books Australia Ltd, P.O. Box 257, Ringwood, Victoria 3134.*

In New Zealand: Please write to *Penguin Books (NZ) Ltd, Private Bag 102902, North Shore Mail Centre, Auckland 10.*

In India: Please write to *Penguin Books India Pvt Ltd, 11 Panchsheel Shopping Centre, Panchsheel Park, New Delhi 110 017.*

In the Netherlands: Please write to *Penguin Books Netherlands bv, Postbus 3507, NL-1001 AH Amsterdam.*

In Germany: Please write to *Penguin Books Deutschland GmbH, Metzlerstrasse 26, 60594 Frankfurt am Main.*

In Spain: Please write to *Penguin Books S. A., Bravo Murillo 19, 1° B, 28015 Madrid.*

In Italy: Please write to *Penguin Italia s.r.l., Via Benedetto Croce 2, 20094 Corsico, Milano.*

In France: Please write to *Penguin France, Le Carré Wilson, 62 rue Benjamin Baillaud, 31500 Toulouse.*

In Japan: Please write to *Penguin Books Japan Ltd, Kaneko Building, 2-3-25 Koraku, Bunkyo-Ku, Tokyo 112.*

In South Africa: Please write to *Penguin Books South Africa (Pty) Ltd, Private Bag X14, Parkview, 2122 Johannesburg.*